Loyalty Unleashed II:

More Pit Bulls and the People Who Love Them

Sue Torres

To all who believe in equality and who strive daily to make it a reality, to anyone who has ever adopted/loved a shelter pet and to animal lovers everywhere. We are all in this together.

"We cannot do great things on this Earth, only small things with great Love." ~ Mother Teresa

CONTENTS

FOREWORD — Page 9
INTRODUCTION — Page 13
STORIES and PICTURES — Page 15
MICKEY — Page 339
ACKNOWLEDGEMENTS — Page 349

FOREWORD

As you may know, "Loyalty Unleashed: Pit Bulls and the People who Love Them," published in May, 2014, was my first experience with writing a book and all that goes along with it. What you may not know is that my plan to write the book almost never came to fruition. I could never have accomplished my objective without a lot of help and support from my family, my friends in the animal welfare community and others who have already been acknowledged and know who they are. Most of all though, I could not have done it without the incredible dogs whose stories were detailed in the book and their loving humans who were kind enough to share them.

I began the project in the summer of 2013. I had no idea where it would lead but, at least in my mind, it was important. On the urging of a family member, I decided to attempt to debunk some of the myths and hysteria surrounding pit bull breed dogs. My aspiration was to create a more positive image of these dogs who are almost universally portrayed in a negative light. I embraced the idea because number one, I have always enjoyed writing, but more importantly because the unplanned adoption of my first pit bull not only changed my life, but enriched it in ways I could never have imagined.

My dog Mickey found me through a picture on a Facebook page. He was rescued with only hours to live and came to live with me and my family on February 25, 2011. I did not actually meet him until after I committed to adopting him but, in my typical idealistic way, I proceeded undaunted – convinced that it would all work out in the end. Somehow I just knew he was meant to be mine.

Mickey's story, prior to the day he entered my life, is one I will never know. Based on his demeanor when he first arrived, I can only try to imagine what he had endured. I had adopted dogs with unknown pasts before, but this was uncharted territory. Mickey came with baggage I was not sure I was equipped to handle. It was an arduous process to teach him to trust and build his confidence but we stuck with it. As Mickey and I forged ahead and evolved together, what I discovered underneath all the bravado and the fear was one of the sweetest dogs in the world – with people of all ages and dogs of all breeds, shapes and sizes. It was a long and often challenging roller coaster ride, but it was worth every minute. I would do it again in a heartbeat.

Adopting Mickey has been quite an eye-opening experience for me. He has taught me things I would never have otherwise learned. Mickey has taught me tolerance and patience. He has taught me volumes about dog training and behavior, to the point where now people sometimes come to me for advice. Imagine that!

Most importantly, Mickey has inspired me to be an advocate for him and for other dogs like him. I wrote "Loyalty Unleashed" with the goal of helping others learn what Mickey has taught me – that it is not the look of a dog that matters but what is inside. He has taught me the true meaning of unconditional love. I could never have predicted how much this one dog would so profoundly influence my life.

While I thought I was doing a good deed by giving an unwanted death row dog a home, what he wound up giving me was so much more. What Mickey gave me was his heart. I am not sure who got the better end of the deal. What I do know is that we both won.

Like Mickey, every dog has a story to tell and I was presented the opportunity to share a few of them. I wanted to chronicle the lives of some of the dogs the mainstream media wanted to categorize and malign as a group, instead of seeing each one as an individual. Two of my passions – writing and dogs – converged. The result was "Loyalty Unleashed: Pit Bulls and the People Who Love Them," a collection of over one hundred happy pit bull rescue/adoption stories from around the country.

It was a surreal feeling when I saw my book available online for the first time. I thought, "I did it – I made it to the finish line!" Except it was not the end. It was just the beginning. What followed was a year filled with book signings, events, speaking engagements and so much more. Most recently I have become involved in the political process in my state, hoping to help change some of the existing and antiquated laws and give animals a better existence.

I have also fostered several dogs since the book came out, in large part because of contacts I made through my book. Fostering is a most rewarding experience and knowing that these former shelter dogs now have wonderful, loving homes has been the greatest reward of all.

"Loyalty Unleashed" made all of this possible. What began with a simple idea progressed into an incredible journey filled with travel, extraordinary and compassionate people and of course magnificent pit bulls with loving hearts. It is a journey I will continue with excitement, enthusiasm and anticipation.

Thank you all for making it possible.

INTRODUCTION

When I finally completed work on "Loyalty Unleashed," perhaps my only regret was that I was not able to include pictures of all of the dogs in the book. I was limited to a finite number of photographs and having to eliminate so many beautiful pictures was the most difficult part of the entire process. I hope those who did not have pictures accompanying their stories will understand my dilemma, but the good news is that now I have a chance to make amends!

Now I have the opportunity to display many more pictures, reveal some updates and share some new material as well. In this book, you will see photographs of the original dogs (both old and new), hear how some of the dogs are doing now, get to know the hero dogs that have been featured on my website (for those who may have missed them the first time around) and meet some new dogs and their owners too.

It is with great pleasure and excitement that I introduce to you "Loyalty Unleashed II: More Pit Bulls and the People Who Love Them."

STORIES AND PICTURES

"The world would be a nicer place if everyone had the ability to love as unconditionally as a dog."
M.K. Clinton

"Dogs, for a reason that can only be described as divine, have the ability to forgive, let go of the past, and live each day joyously. It's something the rest of us strive for." ~ Jennifer Skiff

MONTHLY HERO MOO - THANKS TO LAUREL COX

As a volunteer for the City of Hartford Animal Shelter, I see a lot of dogs that tug at my heartstrings. But in July of 2013 there was one that didn't just tug, but grabbed on and would not let go.

Moo was a blind, thin, senior pit bull that had been found roaming the streets of Hartford. Despite how scared and confused she must have been, she had nothing but tail wags and kisses for anyone who showed her attention. While the rest of the kennels were filled with younger dogs, I knew she had many strikes against her. I could not let her die. I networked her, I visited with her and when it got close to her last day, I realized she was not going to die because I was going to be the one to take her home.

The evening I pulled her from the pound, I slept on the floor with her. It was not until that time that I realized how very sick she was. However, she curled up with her head on my shoulder and slept so deeply and soundly that I wondered when her last good night of sleep had been. The next morning I brought her to the vet and despite her condition, she greeted everyone with exuberance. She immediately won over the hearts of everyone in the office. After an initial examination, the vet told me with tears in her eyes that Moo was very sick and that she would do everything she could for her.

I left her in the capable hands of my trusted vet but with a pit in my stomach. Moo was diagnosed with diabetes, pyometra, advanced cataracts and major skin infections. We tackled one issue at a time and to watch this dog who had been through

SO much continue to smile and love everyone she encountered was so inspirational to me. She would give kisses while getting an injection of insulin. I don't know how long Moo had lived in this condition, but I do know that she never let it get to her. Her blindness bothered me more than it bothered her. She just appreciated a home, regular meals and most of all constant love and attention. She relished in the good things and did not let the bad things get her down. We should all learn from this behavior.

Once Moo's health had improved, it was time to visit an animal eye care specialist. Now that her eyes were no longer red and oozing with the course of eye medication, there was the possibility that she would be a candidate for cataract surgery and potentially have some sight restored. How thrilled I was after her initial consult and tests to find out she could have this surgery!

In May, nine months after she left the dog pound with me, Moo had the miracle of sight restored. The first time she truly saw me, she didn't know I was her mom until I spoke. And then her tail wagged and she ran to me. It was an amazing thing to witness, and it continues to be an amazing journey to watch.

Everything is new to her. While her quality of life has certainly improved, her personality has never changed. She had as much love and zeal for life when she was blind as she does now with sight.

I have always known Moo is a special dog; a brave, courageous soul with a heart big enough to love the world. It was not until recently that I realized she also has a story to tell, lessons to teach, people to heal. She senses when people are sad and she is drawn to them and will immediately, gently put her head against them.

She visited a group of three to six year olds at a school and brought smiles to all the children's faces as she used my voice to explain that being different is okay, to always accept people for who they are and the things that make us different are the things that make us special. I heard from a parent that those kids talked about Moo for days.

Moo and I will continue her journey. She was meant to be in my life and I was meant to be in hers. When I want to start complaining about the smallest of things, I think of Moo. She has made me a better person.

When I take her to the park she takes everything in - a flower, a leaf blowing across the grass, a child playing. She stops, she

stares and I swear she smiles. She has taught me to appreciate the smallest of joys and I will forever be grateful to this amazing dog for teaching life lessons to everyone who has the privilege of meeting her. Moo is my HERO!

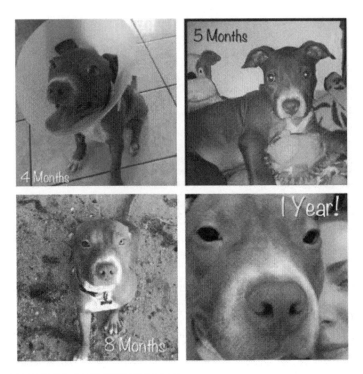

FAUSTO (ADRIEN ZAP)

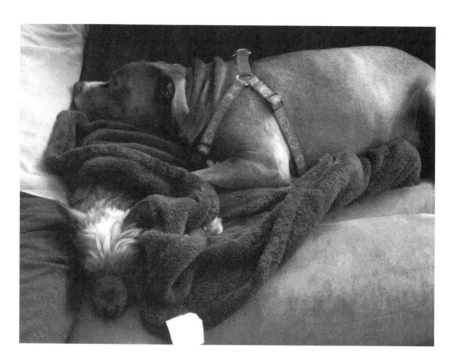

BUBBA (TRACEY PETRY)

WAKEFIELD – THANKS TO DAVID DUFAULT

This story begins in rural Mississippi where I was stationed with the Navy in 2010. It starts with a skinny and scarred dog rooting through a bag of trash on the side of a winding road. It is impossible to know what the poor beast had been though before our story starts, whether it was willful abuse or just the passive and pervasive neglect so many unwanted animals endure. It was horrible though, whatever it was. To this day I am grateful my path crossed that dog's path.

I was driving home from work on a spring afternoon and saw at a distance what I thought was a buzzard picking through a bag of garbage waiting for collection on the side of the road. As I passed, I realized it was not a buzzard at all. The creature was all bony joints and bulging ribs; a bald, skinny thing that as I looked closer turned into a dog. My stomach turned, and I looked away quickly when I realized what it was.

It is tempting to do nothing in situations like that. I do nothing all the time, and I almost did nothing then too. It is easy to say to ourselves:

> *"I just got off work and want to go home"*
> *"Someone else will take care of it"*
> *"It's not my problem"*

We see awfulness every day, that we overlook or push out of our minds to save ourselves from discomfort and inconvenience. I am the same way, and I can't say what compelled me to do something that day. In the rural South, seeing stray or neglected animals is common. It is so common that it dulls you to the experience. Having never seen a dog so wretched before must have been what shook me to act that day.

I wanted to do something, but I did not know what that something should be. Food was a good place to start though, so I went to the nearest convenience store, picked up a bag of puppy food and crossed my fingers that the dog would be there when I got back. The road is winding and green, with narrow drainage on either side and forest beyond. It is lush and dense enough that I knew if he had moved back in the woods, I likely would never find him again. Fortunately for us both, the dog was still there nosing though the rubbish for scraps.

I pulled off the road close to where he was and approached slowly to make sure I didn't startle him into running off. As I walked up he turned to face me, wagged his tail a couple times and gingerly lowered himself on his haunches. I got my first good look at him then and he was a horror to say the very least. Open cuts lined his face and legs. He was missing most of his hair and was skinnier than any living thing should be. A filthy, large collar hung around his thin neck. His ragged skin was covered in ticks and his limbs were swollen. His eyes were nearly caked shut with filth. He smelled like rot.

Can you imagine smiling through something like that? I complain about a bum ankle and occasionally let the sports page ruin my day. However, here was this animal literally on death's door who put his ears back and wagged his tail when I said, "Hi, buddy." Every move he made must have caused him considerable pain.

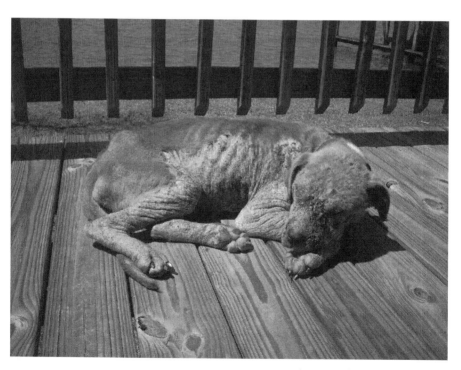

I put the bag of food down in front of him and thought about what to do next as he ate. If I left him there with the food he would still almost certainly succumb to starvation later. If I picked him up he might be less than appreciative, and he was so disgusting that the thought of touching him to get him in my car was giving me some pause. I decided to take my usual path when faced with a difficult decision and called my wife Lisa, who sagely and unsurprisingly told me to just do what I thought was right.

I knew what was right in this case, so after some cajoling and pleading (and an attempted escape under a nearby barbed wire fence) I was able to get him into my car and to a nearby and trusted veterinarian's office. On the way, I spoke calmly and told him I would look after him, but in my mind I was certain the vet would want to put the dog to sleep and end his misery. I dropped him off, said goodbye to the still nameless and hairless monster and tried to make some peace with the idea that it was okay if all I had done was give him a quick and painless end.

That being said, it was with much surprise that I received news from the vet's office that:

1. It was hard to tell what age or breed of dog he was due to his physical condition, but the doctor's best guess was that he was a six to eight month old pit bull.

2. The dog was starving and riddled with ticks and infection but might survive. His primary issue was an extreme case of Demodex mange, but aside from that he did not have any terminal conditions. He was dreadfully sick, but although he might still die there was nothing guaranteeing that outcome. Since he was "mine" at that point, the vet told me I could either have him put down or I could give him a chance at recovery.

The first thing I heard was "he might make it."

The second thing I heard was "pit bull."

I balked at the idea of having a pit bull in the house. All I knew about pit bulls was what the newspapers told me: *They fight. They're vicious.* This was before I became aware of the wide world of pit bull love and advocacy that exists (that would come later). Fears about his breed were secondary though; after the vet said he had a chance I knew I had to see that chance through. After a thorough check up, vaccinations, a tick bath and what I can only imagine was an elephant's dose of antibiotics at the vet's office, I loaded the sorry animal in my car and took him home.

The dog's first couple of days home were spent alternating between wolfing down whatever food I put in front of him and sleeping in a tight little ball on his bed. He ate almost ten full cups of food that first day and was so tired that when I picked him up to go to the bathroom he barely stirred. At one point I thought he was having a bad dream, but upon closer inspection I realized the movement I witnessed was a tick exodus. The vet's office had taken many ticks off of him and the bath he received gave the rest a lethal dose of meds. That first night the stragglers were crawling off his body in droves. I don't remember how many I captured or pulled off of him, but I think dozens is probably in the ballpark.

As I watched him eat and rest that first day I could tell he was a fighter. Not a fighting dog, but a dog with a lot of fight. He ate like he wanted to live. He still needed a name though, so I named him after one of my all time favorite baseball players, Tim Wakefield.

Since this is a story about a dog and not a story about baseball, I will be brief: Tim Wakefield is a hero among Red Sox fans. He will never be in The Baseball Hall of Fame in Cooperstown.

He might not be remembered by many outside the rabid Boston fan base. He pitched in a losing effort against the Yankees in the playoffs in 2004, volunteering to take the mound in a game that was already sure to be a loss. He took his lumps but saved the bullpen, allowing the Red Sox to mount the greatest comeback in sports history the following game. He had guts. How do you step up in an already losing effort, knowing you are going to get pounded in front of millions of viewers?

This dog had guts too. How else do you wag your tail when you are covered in sores and starving? He didn't just need food and care, he needed a name that would give him a leg up. A name that the universe had already deemed worthy. So Wakefield it was.

I was hopeful but not terribly optimistic about his chances in spite of the good name during his first week with me. He was eating a ton and wagging his tail when I spoke to him, but he spent most of his time sleeping. I worried over him constantly and rushed home during lunch breaks and after work to make sure he was still alive.

My first real assurance that he was turning a corner came at the end of that first week. I sat outside the laundry room where he was shacked up and called his name, trying to get him to come out of bed under his own power and walk around. He did, in what I can only describe as a moment almost too sappy to be real. He walked over to me, shaky, head and tail lolling a little as he did. He sat down beside me and put his still swollen paw in my lap. I couldn't really pet him because of the condition of his skin, so I gently put my hand on the back of his neck (the only place he still had all his hair) and told him I would do whatever it took to get him the good life a dog deserves. Sniffles, right?

After that first week his recovery was dramatic. He ate so much food that his weight gain was daily noticeable. As his ravaged body put on weight and rested, it healed. After another week his eyes, which would every morning be caked shut with infection crud, cleared up completely. His many sores started to scab over and his angrily swollen legs and paws started to look normal. Instead of having to be carried outside he started leading me on the leash to sniff around. Watching a creature recover from such a broken place was a joy. It had its moments for sure. When he would do what my wife and I call the "doggy shake it off" he would send disgusting goop flying all over the place. When his body started to de-worm, well, I will leave that to the imagination if you feel the need to visualize it.

I had no idea that as a normal part of the recovery from such a severe case of mange the poor guy would lose all of his hair. For a while he was in a gargoyle phase; he was getting plump and healthy, but without hair he looked like the Hellhound from Ghostbusters. Watching such a creature pounce on a tennis ball is quite the laugh.

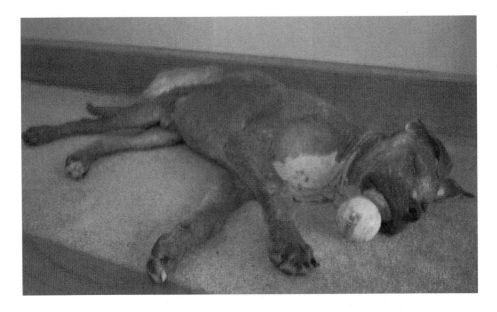

As Wakefield convalesced with me down in Mississippi, my wife and I started making a plan to introduce this pit bull to our other two dogs. While I worked with the Navy in Mississippi, my wife worked in Arkansas.

I spent weekends at our home north of Little Rock and left Wakefield at the vet's office when I was gone. When he reached the "no longer contagious" portion of his recovery from the mange it was time to bring him home.

Fingers were crossed (both hands and my toes too) that he would get along with our pack. By this time I knew Wakefield was a terrific dog; he loved everyone he met. He had yet to interact with other dogs though, and there was this "pit bull" thing to worry about. Would he bite? Would he be aggressive? Would he submit to our VERY alpha beagle that ruled the roost?

We did our research, and after looking carefully through the hype and hysteria the media peddles about pit bull attacks we were able to separate the wheat from the chaff. Awesome organizations like BAD RAP and The Unexpected Pit Bull opened our eyes to the reality about bullies - they are just dogs like any other breed. The "inherently dangerous" label is a fiction. Breed Specific Legislation targeting pit bulls is a convenient but wrong-headed fix to the problem of dog attacks.

When we introduced Wake to the rest of our pack, he made fast friends with our dogs. This scabbed and plump pup ran and played, and being the low man on the doggy totem pole showed his belly to keep the peace when he needed to.

He officially became a forever member of the family right then and there.

It has been a wonderful and hilarious five years with Wake under our roof. He grew and grew and finally settled in at around eighty pounds of blockhead and muscle. He still has scars on his legs and head where the worst of the wounds were located. He occasionally gets lumps and bumps that come and go, or he will lose a small patch of hair just to find it again a month later.

He is an incredibly loving member of our family, both to Lisa and me, all the guests and company that visit us and to the near-constant rotation of foster dogs that come and go though our door.

Wake knows how to wrestle and rough-house with the big dogs we have helped and he knows how to gently mouth play with the puppies that have spent time with us.

His calm and kind demeanor have helped us rehabilitate dogs with severe anxiety. He is a true ambassador for the breed and I can't help but think he changes minds about pit bulls every time he gives a new person a kiss with his extra large tongue.

This story that started so sad on that rural road five years ago has a happy ending. Wakefield is living the high life with Lisa, me and the rest of our pack in Southern California, lazing his days away in the sun.

He and I are lucky we found each other: I got him back to health, and he got me out of the rut of complacency and inaction. I am grateful to Wakefield for forcing me to *do something*. For helping me to ignore those selfish voices inside that told me it was not my problem. It *was* my problem. No one was coming along after me to patch him up.

There is a wonderful quote by Lily Tomlin that perfectly sums up that sentiment and informs how I hope to live my life:

"I always wondered why somebody doesn't do something about that. Then I realized I was somebody."

LUCKY (LAURA CLARK)

MEA (AMIE ARDITI)

COCO (UPDATE) THANKS TO TAMMY CONNELLY

Coco is now four years old. We have had her for three years and she just became a big sister! We had a baby boy on November 8, 2014 and she has been nothing but wonderful with him. She is a little mother hen always checking in on him and wanting to be close to him. She loves to rest her head on him when I am feeding him.

We are hoping that one day Coco will be a Therapy Dog. We are not there yet but we are making progress.

We are still working on some leash training and curbing her jumping and high energy level, but Coco is proof that in the right environment pit bulls are nanny dogs and are excellent with children.

DELILAH (KAREN SCHIFFMAN)

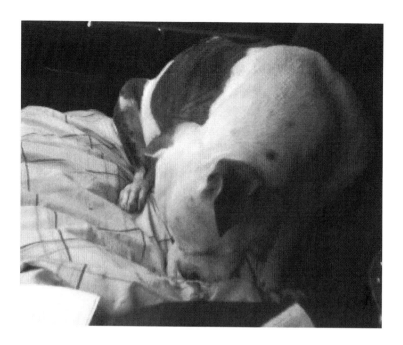

ROSIE (CATHY CLARK)

"Dogs have given us their absolute all. We are the center of their universe. We are the focus of their love and faith and trust. They serve us in return for scraps. It is without a doubt the best deal man has ever made. " Roger A. Caras

BUDDY (LESLIE POLIAK)

MONTHLY HERO JACKSON – THANKS TO SHANNON GRAHAM

I was always *that* person – the one who believed all the media hype. I would tell my husband there was no way EVER that we were getting a pit bull. We had two Rottweilers and a Shih-Tzu. I said I would never trust a pit bull and I would not have one around our family. It is actually really embarrassing to admit that I was a sheep that followed the media hype.

Then one day I heard that a family member bred her female pit bull to make some money (ugh!!!) As if that was not bad enough, she couldn't sell all of the puppies and was looking to find homes for the two that nobody wanted. I agreed to "just look" at them.

She brought over two black puppies. I remember thinking, "they don't look vicious," and being surprised that they looked like normal, cute, cuddly puppies. I could not resist.

That day I chose Jackson. I did not know at the time that he would literally change my life.

As I got to know Jackson, my love for him grew beyond what I thought I would ever feel for an animal. Sure I loved our other dogs, but Jackson was special. He was smart as a whip. He learned so many tricks in a matter of minutes! He loved to just snuggle with me and shower me with kisses. All he wanted was my love, and very quickly he had it.

When Jackson was about a year old, I decided that I wanted to help other dogs like him - dogs who were judged before they were ever given a chance to prove people wrong. Jackson inspired me to become an advocate for pit bulls; to be their voice. He inspired me to become a safe place for other pit bulls to wait until they could find their forever families. He inspired me to become involved in rescue, to foster and to save lives.

Jackson inspired me to become fiercely protective of the breed I once hated. He inspired me to look at my own ignorance, to become more compassionate, patient, accepting and loyal.

I will forever be grateful to my gorgeous Jackson for teaching me so many lessons and inspiring me to go out and educate others about this loyal, loving, resilient and misunderstood breed.

I am a better person today because of Jackson. He is truly my hero.

BOCEPHUS and DAISY (AMANDA CRITTENDON)

SOLDIER (HEATHER KOHLER)

WALTER (MARCI BALONICK)

LINDA (UPDATE) - THANKS TO KELLY TURNBULL

Linda is now ten years old and doing well. We lost our other dog, Linda's best friend in December, 2014. After a couple of very difficult months mourning his loss, we met our most recent foster - a bulldog mix named Winston. Winston has been such a perfect addition to our family that we decided to make him a permanent member and adopted him in May. Winston has put spunk into Linda again and she now plays like a puppy with him. Unfortunately, due to the pit bull ban in Ontario where we live, we are unable to rescue another pit bull but we are happy to welcome Winston into our family.

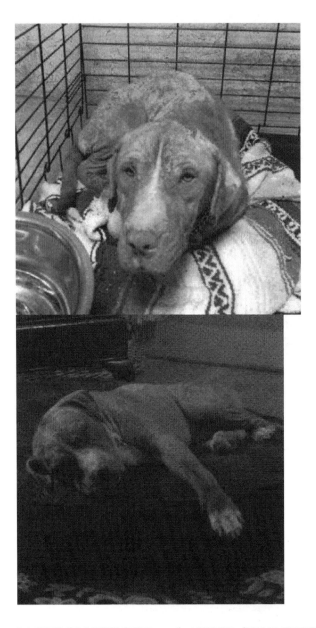

JACKSON BEFORE and AFTER (JENNIFER THOMPSON)

BUDDY (CAITLYN DALTON)

RESCUED IN PETUNIA THE PIT BULL'S MEMORY –
PENELOPE AND LOLA (JENNIFER COOLEY)

MONTHLY HERO KARMA – THANKS TO LISAMARIE SAPP

One day I received a phone call from a friend who is very involved in rescue. She was calling to tell me that while she was waiting at the vet's office, there was a young man with a pit bull puppy in the waiting room with her. As she sat there, she watched him "discipline" his puppy by hitting and kicking him.

My friend introduced herself and told the young man that if he was feeling overwhelmed, she could help find a home for the dog. He told my friend that he also had a female at home but was not interested in getting rid of either one of them. Lo and behold, he had a change of heart and called her later that day offering to surrender the female.

I immediately got a phone call asking if I could foster the puppy until we could find her a good home. My husband was not happy but my daughter and I promised to actively help look for a home for her. I picked her up on a Friday afternoon and brought her to a street fair the very next day so she could get out and meet some people. I was convinced that finding her a home would not be difficult. After all, her face was irresistible.

As I expected, people fell in love with her at the street fair and I came home with quite a few phone numbers. I told people I would contact them but I had to check references first. I was excited to tell my husband about all of the interest in this puppy. As my daughter and I started to tell him about our day, he stopped us and told us it was no longer necessary to look for a home for her because he had already found one. When I asked, "With whom?" he responded, "US!" So in less than twenty-four hours, we were "foster failures" and we had ourselves a new puppy.

Now it was time to start training her. When I first brought her home she flinched if you moved too quickly and she cowered down if voices were raised, even when in excitement. I immediately changed her name to Karma (good karma of course) and took her somewhere every day to socialize her. I enrolled her in obedience classes and in a few weeks she got her Puppy Good Citizen Award.

As we continued in obedience classes my trainer would put Karma next to the more difficult dogs. She seemed to balance them. Karma is the type of dog you can take anywhere and not worry.

One of the ladies I work with had a Lab that she would take to run on a local trail. I thought Karma would enjoy hiking with another dog so I asked if we could meet there one day. My co-worker was very hesitant because Karma was a pit bull.

Trusting my experience with dogs she reluctantly agreed. I brought Karma to the trail and Karma and Murphy played all day. My colleague still tells me how Karma completely changed her opinion about pit bulls.

Karma has that effect on people. Initially they are afraid of the breed, but then they meet her and fall in love with her.

Fast forward two years and I received another phone call from my friend about a Bulldog/pit mix in North Carolina. This guy was hit by a car and left for dead. His front leg was broken in multiple places, he had a collapsed lung, was heartworm positive and had some vision issues. How could I

say no? We brought him to our home after rehab in Tennessee and from the minute he met Karma they were inseparable! His name is Cupid and it turns out he is completely blind. Karma is always with him and acts as his eyes. She will settle down right by him every night.

When they go outside, if she doesn't stay near him she always comes back to check on him. Cupid doesn't like most dogs, including my other two at times, but he has never even growled at Karma. You can tell how much he loves her.

Karma is my hero, overcoming the rough start she got in life. She is the most lovable, balanced dog I know.

After getting Cupid and watching her interact with him. I know she is not only a hero to me, but to Cupid as well.

TIFFANY and CHARLIE (JEROMY McFARREN)

JASMINE (SUSAN SCHIAVONE)

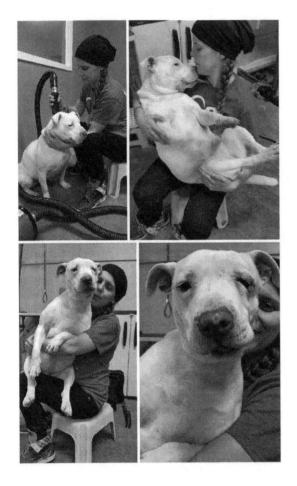

DAGNY (RAFI JOHNSON, WILLY'S HAPPY ENDINGS and SEAN CASEY ANIMAL RESCUE)

WALTER, RUPERT and UPDATES FROM THE REEERANCH - THANKS TO DONNA CODYKO

Walter

Walter - my love, my doggie, my soul mate - is doing great. He is spoiled rotten. He loves every creature that walks through the door and is the best dog I have ever had the honor of being owned by. I love all my kids but there is a bond we share that is so unique, there are no words - it just shows.

I am sad to say that Rupert crossed the bridge this past May. He was silly, goofy and very childlike. He loved to watch videos on tablets or phones which is funny enough in itself, but he actually asked you to turn them on! He also had a He also had a girlfriend here, Baby. She is a sweet, shy Vizsla mix who joined us this past year.

Rupert is buried here at the ReeeRanch – the only real home he ever knew.

Rupert and Friends (top) and Baby

Last fall, Walter, my Jack Russell Jack and I decided to go out for ice cream. We got about two miles from the farm on the two lane highway when I noticed two dogs running around.

I knew they were not locals because I know every dog that lives within a five mile radius and these two were not from here.

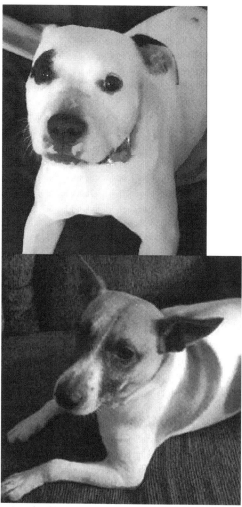

Maybelline (top) and Don Juan

I pulled over and asked a man if they were his. He responded "no" and said that he was trying to catch them so they would not be hit by a truck.

That was when I realized the two were a pit and a Jack Russell! Seriously? I had one set in my car already and now I was about to pick up another. What are the chances of that?

I dropped Walter and Jack off at home and went back to collect these two. The pit bull was a young female, about nine months old and in heat.

She was white with dotted ears and one black eye. I named her Maybelline because she looked like she'd had a run-in with a mascara brush, plus this is Kentucky after all.

The Jack Russell was not neutered and I named him Don Juan (aka DJ) for all the smooth moves he was trying on Maybelline. They had been dumped.

I took them home for baths and flea treatments and I placed a lost and found ad. After three days and no calls it was off to the Bowling Green Humane Society. They received their respective spay and neuter, microchips and shots while there.

After the required five days at the shelter and five days of me actually missing these two little, very bonded goofballs, off to Bowling Green I went to bring home two more furry kids who touch my heart.

They would have a home for the holidays, including our traditional festive turkey dinner.

These two are so bonded. They eat together and sleep together but are both warming up to the rest of the ReeeRanchers nicely.

They are absolute bundles of comedic energy. Maybelline thinks the couch is a trampoline and DJ likes to launch off the recliner. I believe they can fly.

We lost Buddy the day after Christmas, our senior Good Ole Boy – R.I.P. sweet man.

Buddy

Our pack also includes Gabby and seniors Krissy (age twelve) and Woobie (age ten).

As you can well imagine, there is never a dull moment on the ReeeRanch!

Krissy and Gabby (top) and Woobie

CARLIE MASHED POTATOES (KATHIE WEINBERG and
HOME SWEET HOME RESCUE)

SABLE (LAUREN THOMAS)

WALLACE – THANKS TO CAROLINE WILDFEUER

Social media has its good and bad sides when it comes to animals and the rescue world. So, last December when a particular picture caught my eye of a dog in need, an internal buzzer sounded. "Don't even look any further," I told myself. But I followed the orange lead in the picture to the dog's neck and then it happened - the dog and I locked eyes. I did not listen to the internal buzzer and continued down to the story below the picture.

This older fellow had wandered up onto a woman's property. He was good with animals and very sweet but the woman could not keep him. He needed a Christmas miracle or he would have to go to Animal Control by the end of the week.

Without even thinking, I found myself typing, "If no one claims or steps up, we will take him." Then I prayed super hard that someone would. About five days later that someone was me.

This male, stinky dog was brought to me and my daughter as soon as we pulled into the driveway. He jumped right into my little Nissan and never looked back.

Our first stop was the vet where we learned some things about the dog my daughter had already named Wallace.

He was estimated to be about eight to ten years old, although he may be even older.

He tested negative for heartworm, however the tumors which hung from his body appeared to be cancer.

We would find out more when they were removed. He was not neutered and the possibilities were that he could have been used for breeding, may have been fought or hit by a car, or perhaps he just had a rough life.

His teeth (both top and bottom) appeared to have been filed. There was not much else to add but that was more than enough to start with.

There was no sense in waiting so we scheduled the mass removals for the same time as his neuter. Then, after he received his vaccinations, we would bring Wallace home.

We later learned that the tumors were Mast Cell Cancer. So far we have been fairly fortunate as only two more tumors have appeared and they have been removed immediately.

I cannot say enough about Wallace and the love that shines through his eyes, even when he has done something naughty.

"Look mom! I kept busy while you were gone and chewed the molding off the wall!"

He has learned to pull my purse off the counter and then walk through the house with it as if to say, had I taken him with me the first time there would still be trim around the door.

His eyes have allowed me to see the hurt of his past which has transcended into a love for me that is evident to all.

My love for Wallace is comparable to nothing else.

As he listens to my songs and my heart which I share freely with him, I can see to the depths of his soul and feel the gratitude of the dog that I am fortunate enough call mine.

By allowing Wallace to sample all the things he has probably missed out on, I have been given an opportunity to see things through a new set of eyes, to realize that I had been missing out too.

We take long walks in the park and we all of a sudden stop, drop and roll, breathing in the sights and sounds of the world which surrounds us.

We have quiet times where we just stare up at the sky and I realize the grace that has been freely given to the both of us.

I look at him and say "Wallace with all your imperfections you are so perfect. It was not I, my friend, who was your blessing, it was you who was mine. You were MY Christmas miracle."

https://www.facebook.com/pages/Wallace-the-abandoned-Elderbull/1375896496042172?fref=ts

COLONEL – R.I.P. May 22, 2015 (ALLY OLIVER)

BELLA - BEFORE and AFTER (KACI STOKLEY)

MONTHLY HERO LEIA – THANKS TO NANCY MOREHOUSE

Having grown up with dogs, I always wanted one of my own. When my boyfriend and I moved into a two-family home, we learned that our neighbors fostered rescue dogs. I knew right away I was in trouble, but now I had to convince my boyfriend that we needed a dog in our lives.

My boyfriend agreed that fostering would be okay. After all, we wouldn't have to keep the dog! Well then, Leia (called Fern) came to us one day last August. I fell in love with her immediately. My boyfriend did not have quite the same reaction, especially since he came home from work in the middle of the paperwork to find this strange dog relieving herself all over our new, white bedroom carpet. Oops.

However, after a rocky first week, it did not take long for his love affair with her to take off.

Leia is a pit bull mix of some sort. She had been used for breeding and probably had never known real love in her life.

When we got her, she had just weaned a litter of pups and wound up in a shelter when she was no longer useful. She missed her pups and was not loving the shelter life much. She was energetic but in spite of what she had been through, she was sweet as could be.

It never occurred to either of us that her breed was an issue. We were pretty fortunate because our neighbors had pit bulls and our landlord did not care.

Still, it presents its challenges from time to time. When we are out in public, I am constantly having to defend her breed to people who have never met her.

Leia does her part to dispel the stereotypes. She is well behaved and friendly to all she meets.

My mom watches her all day when I am at work and Leia and my mom's rescue Lhasa mix miss each other on the weekends. My dad plays ball with her every morning and snowshoes with her in the winter.

My nieces and nephew spend hours playing ball with her when they visit, and she watches over them like any nanny dog should.

My boyfriend's parents buy more gifts for her than they buy us. In fact, his mother was concerned when I told her we were getting a pit bull. She had heard so many bad things about them, but it only took one meeting with Leia and his mom is now a pit bull advocate herself. That is what Leia does - she sets a fine example and changes minds, one person at a time.

Leia has become a part of our little family and the extended family. In spite of his initial trepidation, my boyfriend now often chooses her over me. I don't mind though because I know she is the better cuddle buddy.

Leia has created so much joy in my life that sometimes I think my heart might explode. She needed a village to raise her, to train her, exercise her, discipline her and love her. She is a lot of work sometimes, but I think that the best things in life usually are.

Leia had to overcome a rough start in life but she never let it get her down. She amazes us every day with her never-ending zest for life, her perpetual joy and her infinite love.

She teaches people every day that, as with people, dogs should be judged as individuals and that we are all capable of overcoming obstacles when given the chance to shine. Leia has taught us so much in the short time she has been with us and we are better for having her in our lives. That is why Leia is our hero!

HUEY (top) and SEBASTIAN (CAROL DEMAIO)

"I have found that when you are deeply troubled, there are things you get from the silent devoted companionship of a dog that you can get from no other source." ~ Doris Day

GORDY (DENNIS FRAZIER)

QUINCY (SEANA MORRIS)

VINCENZO, EPITOME DOG RESCUE (UPDATE) -THANKS TO ANGELA LAFRANCE

It has been almost six years since we lost Vincenzo, but his legacy is living strong. Epitome Dog Rescue saves and successfully places an average of forty bully breed mixes each year. These dogs vary in age, personality, temperament and history; but there is one constant. They are all precious beings who deserve to live a good life in homes where they are loved and cherished, just like Vinny did.

Vinny was not the only bully breed with whom I chose to share my personal life. His "brother" Reno, a Lab/Pit Bull mix, is still here and is a complete joy. At the time of Vinny's passing, Reno had been with us for about two years. Reno went into a deep depression after losing his brother. I had never seen a dog grieve before and the reality of his grief affected me too.

All I could really do at the time was to have compassion for him and look for ways to help him.

One of those ways came about soon after Vin's passing when I stumbled across a beautiful, little American Pit Bull Terrier, Celena, who was only three and a half months old at the time.

In her short time on earth, she'd had a very rough life. She was starved and lived under extremely dangerous conditions. Leni (Celena's nickname) had significant issues, but also an innately wonderful personality that blossomed once she learned that humans could be good.

She became Reno's reason to emerge from the grief and mine too.

Reno and Vinny

A couple of years after starting Epitome, Finnegan came into the picture. Vincenzo surely sent Finnegan to me because he knew it would take a special person to understand this sweet, crazy boy. Finnegan is a fabulous Boxer/bully mix, but he is fearful and insecure, wearing his heart on the outside for all to see. Finn insists on showing his love and expects yours in return. He has come a long way with his behavior, but it has taken time and work. The payoff for me is that Finn's loyalty and devotion, much like Vinny's, warm my heart every day.

Celena, Reno and Finnegan

I have also had the honor of fostering many dogs for the rescue. Each one has touched me and taught me lessons that will help me help the next ones. We have been fortunate that many wonderful people have stepped up to be on Epitome's board, foster for us, adopt, donate, support us and share our needs with others. We could not rescue without each and every one of them and we especially appreciate our foster and adoptive parents. Fostering and adopting save lives. The act of opening up your home to give a dog, who otherwise would have died or lived a horrible life, a soft place to land is food for your soul. The life you saved will go on to enrich the lives they touch. You are a positive force in this world.

All aspects of rescue are about making the world a better place; one bully breed ambassador and one adoptive family at a time. It is about putting the truth out there with regard to these amazing and deserving beings.

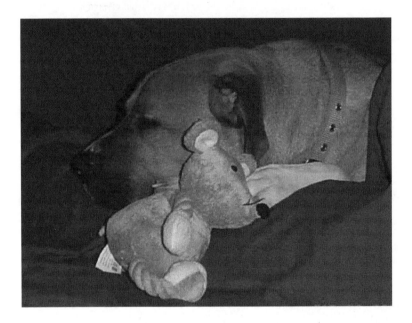

For me, this beautiful cycle began with a gentle, sweet, loving and loyal dog named Vincenzo. I hope everyone can be blessed with a Vincenzo just as I was.

RILEY JAMES and TEAGAN (TAMMY PROP)

ATLAS (CHELSEY FLETCHER)

LUCKY PUPPY – THANKS TO SHARONA KRAVITZ

We waited all day at the Harlem, New York shelter for the driver to bring our newest rescue dog to us from Brooklyn. Many of the dogs my husband and I had previously pulled from that shelter had been sick, mostly with Demodex mange.

This puppy was deathly ill from kennel cough. We knew we could not bring him home that day. We were not even sure he would survive. We left him there, for the shelter vet to treat him, and went home to pray. He was so little, so precious and so sick. My husband and I cried all the way home. Then the waiting began. It was a very long week before we got the call that he could travel home to us on the shelter van. He was a jewel in the rough. He was like a little person. He was home and we adored him but he was not ours to keep. He was a rescue and we knew we had to place him. That was the hard part. We did not know if we could bear to part with him. I named him Lucky Puppy and on to the PetFinder site he went.

We met several families who wanted to adopt this baby boy. I found fault with every single one of them. No one was right. I felt like no one was good enough for him. One day I received an e-mail from a woman in Windsor, Connecticut. She had no other dogs, had just lost her beloved pittie mix and she sounded perfect. I agreed to go to her house to meet her.

When I got there I discovered she was nine months pregnant! I thought, "Oh this is never going to work. She will dump him when the baby comes and she has no time for a puppy." I have seen it happen too many times. I liked her though, and I liked the warmth of her heart, her home and her devotion to pitties. How could I say no?

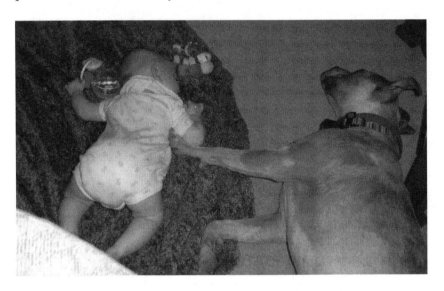

So, with the vet check done, I left part of my heart with her that night. Within weeks, her son Sammy was born and I became part of the family too. I babysat for Lucky Puppy. Sometimes I went there for the night and sometimes he came to us. He was the best body heater ever.

I was still in his life and he was still in mine. I was blessed.

Michele, his new mom, called one day. Lucky had a problem. His fur was falling out. He was going bald. Lucky had a skin condition called ectodermaplasia. His fur was gone and would never come back. He was a bald dog. We would get stopped on the street and people would ask what kind of a dog he was. At the pet expos, Lucky was our ambassador when we helped out at the PetFinder booth. Everyone wanted a Lucky Puppy. He was sort of hypoallergenic!

One day, Lucky, Sammy, Michele and Michele's husband Dick were on their boat on the Salmon River, hanging out near a sand bar. Lucky loved the water. He could swim for hours. A man on the shore yelled at Michele, "Get your pit bull off of my beach!" Well, that was just not going to happen to my Lucky Puppy. Michele came the following weekend and told me the story. My reply to her was, "From now on, he is not a pit bull - he is a rare, hairless, French hunting dog called a LaPete." Well, it stuck! Each time someone asked me what he was, that is what I told them. Most replied "Oh I have heard of that breed but have never seen one!" Michele and I would roll our eyes and try not to laugh. It was our private joke.

Lucky was always a rare breed to me; he was the best rescue dog we ever had. I was blessed to have him in my life for many years. Lucky died last year and my heart was broken, but he resides there forever as the little boy who stole my heart.

I thank Michele every day for allowing me to love him and be near him. He was amazing. He loved baby Sammy with all of his heart. He had the best home and a family that was perfect for him. They loved him until the day he died.

We have rescued many pit bulls and many deeply touched our hearts, but Lucky Puppy was special. He was that one in a million boy that lives on forever.

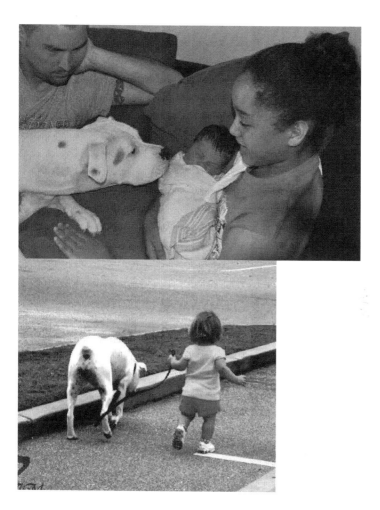

LAYLA (GRADY AND LINDSAY ROUGHTON)

JAIDA and TANK

JAIDA and TANK CONT'D (ELIZABETH KOEGLER)

LILY, LACY and KALI (UPDATE) – THANKS TO KIM BRODASKY

Sadly, my Lily has crossed the bridge. As a result of her abuse, more than half of her life was taken from her. Her kidneys shut down and there was nothing I could do besides watch my baby get sicker until she could no longer fight it.

I had to let her go peacefully, in my home. I miss her terribly and it has not gotten easier as time goes by. I would give my right arm to have more time with her.

In her honor, I rescued a pup. I named her Kali-Lily, after my Lil.

She is a super little girl, but she is still recovering from the neglect she suffered at her first home where she spent her entire life in a crate.

After Lily's passing Lacy was alone. We suffered together and Lacy became depressed and lonely.

Here are some pictures of Lily from her last weekend.

It was only seventeen days after Lily passed that Kali came into our lives and we are doing much better now. I am training Kali to be my PTSD service dog.

Lacy and Kali are inseparable!

"No matter how close we are to another person, few human relationships are as free from strife, disagreement, and frustration as is the relationship you have with a good dog. Few human beings give of themselves to another as a dog gives of itself. I also suspect that we cherish dogs because their unblemished souls make us wish - consciously or unconsciously - that we were as innocent as they are, and make us yearn for a place where innocence is universal and where the meanness, the betrayals, and the cruelties of this world are unknown." Dean Koontz

JAVA (TANYA DENNING)

BRIDGET (FRANCES CARVALHO)

MACY (INSPIRED A CHILDREN'S BOOK – "MACY THE LONELY PIT BULL FINDS A HOME") – THANKS TO TODD JAGEMANN

I have to be honest, when my wife told me that our first dog could be a pit bull mix, I was not thrilled. She called me at work and said there was a dog she found on Petfinder.com that she was really interested in. Immediately, all the bad things you read about and hear on the news went through my mind. "Are you crazy?" I said, "she is going to turn on us, attack our family and friends, we will be sued!" My wife laughed and told me not to believe everything you hear. "Please read her profile that I emailed to you," she said.

Macy was left tied to the front door of a New Jersey shelter. She was in bad shape when the workers found her. She was only thirty pounds, had all types of internal parasites, a prolapsed rectum and scars on her face and paws. Her ears were just about gone, either poorly cropped or the result of possible dog fighting. It would take two surgeries and two months of recovery to get this dog ready for adoption.

Pet Rescue of Mercer was the organization that took on this dog's case. They paid for her recovery and wanted to get her adopted into her forever home. Despite everything she had been through, they said that this dog, now named Angel, still had such a sweet disposition with no ill feelings toward people or other animals.

I did feel sorry for this dog after reading her write-up; however I still was not convinced of how good this breed could be. It took two weeks, two "face-to-dog" meetings and many questions until I finally agreed to give Angel a try. My wife was ready to kill me because she thought someone else would adopt her during that time period. Whether it was fate or just luck, Angel was now ours.

My sister had previously owned a dog named Angel, so we felt the need to change this dog's name. We were struggling to pick a good one so our niece suggested Macy, for her favorite store.

It would take Macy about two months to come out of her shell and be completely comfortable in her new surroundings. She was definitely sweet from the beginning, but she was hand shy (mostly with men), would get startled easily and was not housebroken.

There was one story I remember that broke my heart. It happened the first month we had Macy. I was fixing her Kong with treats and peanut butter one morning when I was getting ready for work. We would give this to Macy when we crated her before we left the house. It was sort of a reward, so Macy would not think of the crate as a punishment.

I remember after the Kong was fixed I put it on a pub chair in our kitchen; I then went into the bathroom. A few moments later I heard this loud bang in the kitchen. I quickly opened the door and rushed out of the bathroom into the hallway. At the same time Macy was running out of the kitchen into the hallway. I did not yell, but I guess there was something she saw in my demeanor because in an instant she hit the ground.

Her tense body was completely flat with her front paws straight out and eyes shut. It looked like she was expecting to get hit and was bracing herself for it.

I got down on the floor and starting reassuring her that everything was fine. I told her "easy girl" while petting her. I then went into the kitchen and realized she must have jumped against the chair. The chair then hit the wall and the Kong fell to the ground. There were treats and peanut butter everywhere.

I literally had to carry Macy back in the kitchen to get her to lick everything up. On this day I think I got a better idea of what this dog must have gone through.

I am thrilled to say that Macy has been with us for about eight years now. She was approximately one to one and a half years old when we adopted her, so we will just say she is almost nine. I cannot believe how fast those years have gone. She has been one of the best dogs we ever had.

Everyone in our family loves her. Even my parents treat her as another grandchild, which is funny, because my mother swore she would never come over again when she first heard we were adopting a pit bull.

Macy loves meeting and playing with other dogs, especially her best friend next door named Jenna who is also a pit bull mix. She loves people, snuggling on cold nights, running in the yard, car rides and going for walks.

Many people have told us that she would make a great ambassador for the pit bull breed. This is when the idea of writing a children's book about her popped into my head.

I was lying in bed early one morning back in March of 2011, when this story starting forming in my head. The story of how we came to adopt Macy.

All of a sudden I had a choice. I could go back to sleep or I could get up and get a pad and paper.

Thankfully, I chose the latter.

I always wanted to write a children's book, but never really had any ideas. Now I had one, and what better way to tell Macy's story than to children. I thought maybe by getting Macy's story out it could change kids' attitudes toward pit bulls, and then possibly adults' attitudes toward this breed would change too. I also wanted to remind them how important pet adoption was.

The story took about three months to complete, which was the easy part. Now the question was, what to do with it? I had never done anything like this before, so I had no clue what to do with this potential children's book. My friend suggested self-publishing, so I decided to look into it.

To make a long story short, the rest of the process took about a year. I had to create a storyboard layout of the book, work with their illustrator on how I wanted the illustrations to look, decide on a cover, the color of the cover, the binding, the size of the pages, etc. It turned out to be a longer process than I thought, but the experience was extremely fun.

"Macy The Lonely Pit Bull Finds A Home" was finally completed in April of 2012. I understand it was not from a major publishing house, but it was still exciting to hold my first book in my hands.

Since that day my wife, Macy and I have done many pro-adoption dog events in our area trying to promote the book, along with some school and other event readings. During all of this, I have come to realize that it is Macy who is the star. Everyone loves meeting her, especially the kids. She loves meeting them too.

We have met so many wonderful people and organizations at these events. We have learned a lot and continue to learn. Of course we have met a lot of great dogs too, many of them pit bulls and there has not been one mean one in the bunch. We also give a percentage of the sale of the book back to Pet Rescue of Mercer and other rescue groups whenever possible. Looking back now it is hard to believe I was so afraid of getting this dog. I have learned so much from Macy and from this journey.

Unfortunately, it is human nature to be judgmental. There are times when we all make judgments about things, sometimes too quickly and most of the time without really knowing the facts. We get caught up in our own lives and do not realize how our actions can affect other people or creatures.

I admit I am far from perfect, but after this experience I try not to judge too quickly anymore. I will leave you with two things that came into my mind while writing this. One is the saying "Don't judge me until you walk a mile in my shoes (or paws)." The other comes from the movie "Evan Almighty": "How do you change the world? With one single act of random kindness."

 https://www.facebook.com/pages/Macy-The-Lonely-Pit-Bull/321747507836679?fref=ts

ROCKY (SYLVIA ELIE)

BROOKLYN (ROBIN RANDALL)

PAIGE (STEPHANIE SLATER)

MONTHLY HERO BETTY BOOP – THANKS TO ANGIE WRIGHT

I have a beautiful story to tell. I have been involved with animal rescue for some time as a volunteer.

When I decided to adopt a dog of my own, my plan was to adopt from an out-of-state rescue. That plan did not work out, so instead I decided to look closer to home and visited a local shelter.

That was where I met Betty Boop. I believe it was serendipity. For me, it was definitely love at first sight.

When I heard she was scheduled to be euthanized the next day, I knew I could not let that happen. I filled out the papers right then and there and, as soon as she was vetted, she came home with me.

Betty Boop had come from a terrible situation. She had been used for breeding and fighting. After I'd had her for two weeks, I also learned that she was heartworm positive and her condition was severe. We were able to raise the money for her treatment and thankfully she pulled through.

I suffer from acute night terrors associated with anxiety and PTSD. Within two days after her arrival, Betty Boop instinctively became aware of my conditions and would awaken me and comfort me at night.

A year later I was diagnosed with several chronic illnesses, one of which is Diabetes. Once again, Betty Boop came to my rescue. Within three months she had taught herself to recognize when my blood sugar is low, which sometimes occurs in my sleep. When this happens she will wake me up and alert me. I can honestly say that without Betty Boop, I might not be here today. I will be forever indebted to this little dog who came into my life when I needed her just as much as she needed me.

Because of the abuse and neglect she suffered before coming to live with me, understandably she can be quite selective when it comes to other dogs. However, this past spring she allowed me to rescue a senior named Mister who had lived for ten years on a chain. It was as though she knew he needed us, and she accepted him into our lives.

In my work as a rescuer, advocate and educator, Betty Boop is my constant companion. She is my best friend. I know she was meant to be in my life and I am grateful every day to have her by my side. She has also been a loving sister and mentor to Mister in his time of need.

In spite of everything she went through before coming home with me, she has been nothing but loving, devoted and grateful for the simple things in life – a roof over her head, a bed, a bowl of food or a hug. I may have given her a home but she has given me so much more than that. She has literally saved my life. Betty Boop is my hero!

Update: Sadly, Mister has crossed the bridge. His last months were spent surrounded by the love of his mom Angie and his canine sister Betty Boop. Angie and Betty Boop continue on their journey together to raise awareness and help other animals in need.

DOLLY (JILL JACOBY)

OPIE (JOE NELSON)

"Dogs are our link to paradise. They don't know evil or jealousy or discontent. To sit with a dog on a hillside on a glorious afternoon is to be back in Eden, where doing nothing was not boring--it was peace." Milan Kundera

SABLE (JEANNIE RENNINGER)

MAMA JADE (CHRISTIANNA WILLIS)

KAYNE (LAURA BIBBEE)

MONTHLY HERO COURAGE - THANKS TO RACQUEL TRAPP, MARY NOVICKY and ANGEL CAPONE PIT BULL RESCUE

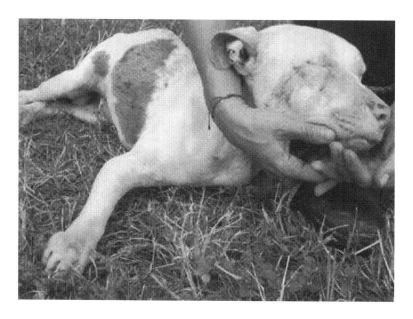

It all started with a text from a Miami Dade Shelter employee on October 28, 2013. Her name was Jesse. She and I had become friendly as we both had the same main goal - saving the bully breeds from Miami Dade.

Jesse wrote, "I know you are full but look at this guy. I think he would be a perfect dog for your hospice foster program. Please look at his pictures. He is getting put to sleep in the morning and he is in horrible shape."

I talked it over with our other volunteers and one, Mary, agreed to take him even though she had current fosters and we were full to the brim with death row dogs we had already rescued. Mary is a health care professional, and nurturing these babies is her specialty. She began as a young girl in Florida, rescuing animals and nursing them back to health – that is what she does.

I messaged Jesse back as I knew time was of the essence and said, "We will take him. Let's get him to a vet down there and get him stabilized for transport up north. We have a home for him for however long he has left."

We received the vet report the next day. It was PAGES LONG. I thought I had seen it all in my years of rescue but I had *never* seen anything like this.

We had already shared his foster plea on our Facebook page, so people were waiting anxiously for a post from us. This was the summary we posted to update everyone on October 29, 2013.

"Courage is one of the worst abuse cases we have ever taken in. His escape from the kill shelter was just the beginning of his battles. He weighs twenty-five pounds. His weight should be double that.

He can barely walk and, according to the shelter partner vet, he has brain damage, shortened long bones, enlarged joints, kyphosis, scoliosis and blackened teeth.

All of this is due to being *severely* malnourished. He was most likely fed just enough to barely survive and kept in a confined space or very small crate his entire life. He is also probably deaf.

He was beaten, but once he realizes your hand is not to hit him he just wants to cuddle in your lap. We realize he will never have a 'normal' life, but we would really like to have the chance to save him and show him what love is.

He is being stabilized right now by our shelter partner's vet and (hopefully) if he is strong enough this weekend, he will get to rest in the comforts of his foster for a couple days. Then, next week, he will have one of the best vets we know managing his care with some of the top specialists in the Northeast."

Many wonderful people stepped up and our rescue was able to raise the necessary funds to give Courage the care he needed. Once stabilized, he made the long trip from Miami to New York.

When he arrived, the first thing he did was to meet his foster mom and what an amazing meeting that was. She came and met him at the transport and it was love at first sight. He just melted into her arms like butter!

The next day it was time. Off to Countryside Vet he went, to get the expert opinion of one of our top vets, Dr. Jim, who explained that this boy definitely had brain damage and needed to immediately get to a Neurosurgeon for stabilization.

Two days later Mary and I took the ferry to one of the best Neurosurgeons in the Northeast, Dr. Infurnuso. He was able to diagnose Courage on the spot. Courage had Cerebellar Ataxia. He may have been born that way and then kept in a cage and abused for being deaf and different, or it may have been a direct result of repeatedly being hit hard on the head.

There is no known treatment for this disease and there are many different grades and forms. The doctor basically said Courage might have months or years left. The immediate need was to focus on stabilizing him and helping him to walk better, so he was not falling and bumping in to walls - and of course to help this poor skeletal dog gain some much needed weight.

One week of decompressing at his foster home was in order and then back to Countryside Vet we went. Courage had a very badly infected mouth. All of his teeth were rotting and they needed to come out.

When a dog is starved for a long time, not only do vital organs and bones get weak, but also the teeth because they were lacking the nutrients to stay strong.

Two weeks later Courage was scheduled for surgery for removal of most of his teeth, treatment of the infections in his mouth and of course a neuter while he was under.

While he stayed at Countryside, the vet techs fell in love with him. He went home on antibiotics and his mommy worked

very hard with him to help him walk better. He was on a liquid diet for some time while his mouth healed and was spoiled beyond belief! After another month he had a photoshoot done by one of our awesome volunteer photographers. Look how much better he looked. By this time he gained at least ten pounds!!

A few months later Courage was finally stable. He would never live a normal life and he was going to always need that extra care, but he started not only walking, but running. And, even though his brain would never understand how to be fully potty trained, he was trying his best to make his mommy happy.

Mary began bringing him to rescue events so he would learn not to be fearful of other humans. He got lots of dog bones (which at first he was afraid of), slept on comfy beds, had a full appetite and was doing just wonderfully. He truly blossomed into a happy dog.

Fast forward almost two years. Mary decided he had come so far with her, it would just set him back if he were placed with anyone else. So he is with her for life!

Mary would like everyone to know how far Courage has come in such a short time. When he first arrived, Courage could not even walk without falling over. Now he runs.

He was totally incontinent and had to be confined to the kitchen. Now he is allowed free reign of the house and has few accidents. It was thought that he would never be able to go up and down stairs or jump up on the furniture. He now does both – like a champ.

Courage used to be terrified of toys and other dogs. He is now part of a pack. He sleeps with the other dogs, plays with soft toys and even plays tug with the other dogs.

He loves baths, car rides, is wonderful with children and enjoys attention of any kind. His favorite thing to do is to cuddle on the couch. Most of all, he has learned to be a dog.

Although he is a little bit "different" there is no reason to believe he will not live as long as any normal dog. He lives for each day and he is one of the most spoiled dogs we have ever met.

Courage has taught us all so much about overcoming pain and obstacles. He has taught us so much about trust and love - about second chances and having a new lease on life. If only humans had the heart of a dog, the world would be a much better place!

BIGGIE (NICOLE MILLETT)

LEXUS (ANGEL GOFF)

"When the Man waked up he said, 'What is Wild Dog doing here?' And the Woman said, 'His name is not Wild Dog any more, but the First Friend, because he will be our friend for always and always and always.'" ~ Rudyard Kipling

ZUKO (ROCCO D'URSO)

KAPPA (UPDATE) - THANKS TO PAT MIGLIORE

Kappa's tail has come to signify the change her life with us has made on her happiness and well-being.

When we adopted her in May of 2013 from the fraternity house where she had lived since she was a puppy, she came into our house behaving like a well-mannered guest.

She was patient, polite, well behaved and took little time to attach to us. Living in a frat house for the first six years of her life had made her into a dog that just "went with the flow." She was well-socialized and people-friendly.

The move to our house probably felt like just another winter break or summer vacation – one of those times when one of the fraternity brothers would take her home while the frat house emptied out for school breaks. She would have a nice vacation in some comfortable new surroundings, ending with a return to the fraternity that might also include some new residents, new furniture and different people coming through.

My husband and I could not help but look her over like new parents and make comparisons to her biological brother Zeppelin, who my son has owned since he was a puppy. Zeppelin is bigger and bulkier, with that classic pit bull block head. I call it "The Wrecking Ball." Kappa's head is smaller and her snout is more tapered. Zeppelin has a white crest on his chest. Kappa is a solid cinnamon color with the exception of her white toes.

But it was the tail. Zeppelin's tail curls up, held high but in a relaxed way, in an almost perfect "C." It gives him an air of confidence, like he feels like he owns the world. Life has been grand for Zeppelin. Six months after Kappa's birth, he was born to the same parents and bought by my son at ten weeks old. Raised in my son Bob's room in the frat house, along with Kappa, Zep was able to leave with Bob when he graduated and moved out. Kappa belonged to the frat and had to stay. Zeppelin continued in a stable life with Bob, ultimately joined by a girlfriend (known as "Mommy") and finally a rescue sibling, Ithaca. All his life he has been loved, fed, run and walked as part of a stable family of four.

Kappa stayed on at the frat house. Year after year there were people moving in and people moving out. It was an endless cycle of getting attached to some of the brothers, only to have them eventually move out and leave her behind to get used to a whole new cast. They loved her but she always lacked stability and constancy.

"Her tail," I observe to my husband soon after getting her, "it sits flat and straight. It just hangs." I thought that was just how she was. Just like one sibling can have a white crest and one not.

Then one day, a month or so after getting her, we were on a walk and I noticed her tail. It was up high, curled in a "C," swinging back and forth happily as she trotted down the road, head held high, with a bounce in her step.

This is *her* neighborhood now. She goes on *her* daily walk with *her* mommy following behind. She has a life that is predictable, with regular exercise, meals, hugs and kisses. She has her own toys, her own blanket and her own bed.

Not a day goes by now that I do not look at her tail during a walk and smile.

MIKO (DANNIE GABBERT)

PIPER, BABE and GP (GOAT PUPPY) – (NATE and JULIE FREE)

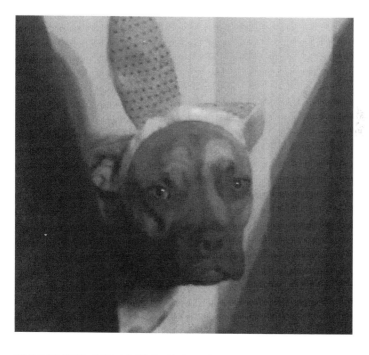

BEECHER (BRANDI BYERS)

"Every dog starts life with a blank canvas. His destiny etched by the hands of the painter, and each one an artist's original. The portrait painted depends on how the brush is held. Paint with hostility, and a dog learns to fight. Paint with cruelty, and a dog learns fear. Paint with anger, and a dog learns aggression. Paint with praise, and a dog learns confidence. Paint with boundaries, and a dog learns respect. Paint with tenderness, and dog learns to bond. Paint with affection, and a dog learns to love. Every dog is a product of its environment. Bad dogs are not born, they are created. If the portrait is flawed, look to the artist. Stop blaming the dogs!" ~ Jodi Preis

SMOKEY (SALLEE HANNON)

MONTHLY HERO RAVIOLI - THANKS TO AMANDA QUICK, GABRIELLE CAMP and KATHERINE CAMP

There are two parts to Ravioli's story. We begin with her rescue by Amanda Quick and her husband.

On January 27, 2013, my husband and I were driving home from having dinner at a local Italian restaurant. As we rounded the last curve before our neighborhood, there stood the most pitiful little dog I had ever seen. She was skin and bones. With ears cropped nearly completely off and a big, square head, there was no doubt she was a pit bull and a badly neglected one at that. We stopped the car to offer her our leftover pasta, but she had other plans and with one agile leap, she sailed right into our back seat. We knew then and there that we had to do whatever we could for this little girl, starting with naming her Ravioli.

The next day we took Ravioli to the vet and were overwhelmed with all that we discovered. She had every intestinal parasite imaginable.

She had several filed and missing teeth, leading us to believe she had been used as a bait dog. She was heartworm positive. And last but not least, she was pregnant.

That night I reached out to every local rescue possible, only to be told repeatedly that no one was willing to help us. I just could not give up on her though, so I started a Facebook page and began posting photos of Ravioli and sharing her story.

What happened next was beyond amazing. Donations started coming in from all over the country and even some from Europe!

We were blessed enough to raise enough money to treat Ravioli for heartworms, get her a dental cleaning and extract her broken and painful teeth, and vaccinate and spay/neuter her and all eight puppies. Over the next year, all of the puppies were adopted out into loving, wonderful homes!

You may not see what is so heroic about Ravioli. She seems like a victim at first glance, not a hero, but rest assured she is both. Through being abused, baited, neglected, repeatedly bred and abandoned to die of heartworms, Ravioli never gave

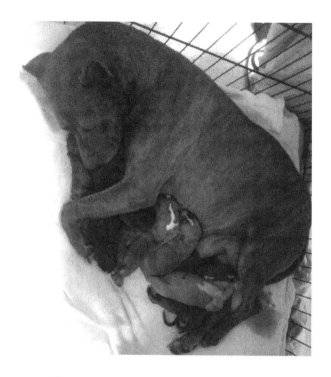

up. Though people neglected and abused her and dogs attacked her, she still trusted both and longed for their companionship. She still saw the good in us when all she had ever known was bad. She loved like no dog I have ever met when all she had ever known was hate. Her story touched so many people that donations continue to come in and we are able to donate those to rescues and charities that have "Raviolis" of their own. We host dog washes and raise money to give back to rescue. When Ravioli needed someone, no one was there, so she found us and she rooted so deeply in our hearts that we cannot help but want to continue raising funds so that we can keep other dogs from feeling the loneliness of neglect and of being a stray. What makes Ravioli a hero above all else is her ability to love those who do not deserve it!

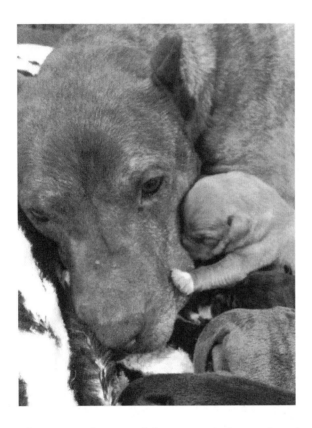

The second part of the story is her adoption by Gabrielle and Katherine Camp.

I first met Ravioli in October of 2013 at the Bark in the Park Atlanta Braves game. Her rescuer, Amanda Quick, had taken Ravi to the game in hopes of meeting some potential adopters. As luck would have it, I ended up sitting beside them and Ravi's story touched my heart so much that I could not let her walk out of Turner Field with no permanent home. I filled out an application right there at the ball park!

Amanda told me how she had found Ravi in January of 2013, running around the streets of Atlanta, lost, confused, sick, hungry and extremely pregnant. Amanda took her into her home and nurtured her back to health.

The day I first saw Ravi, something was still missing - a permanent home. I decided to adopt Ravioli that day but sadly only two days later had to call Amanda to let her know that the neighbors were upset with an "aggressive dog" being in close proximity with their cats.

During the two days that I had Ravi, my sister Katherine absolutely fell in love with her. She was also devastated by the news that I had to return Ravi to Amanda.

During the months to follow, I kept in contact with Amanda to see how Ravioli was doing. I just could not give up on her. Ravi bounced from different "permanent" homes during those months, but sadly only to return to Amanda weeks later. One night in January of 2014, I got a text from Amanda saying that Ravi had been attacked by her dog and was severely injured in the fight.

Everyone was at their wits end trying to find Ravi a safe home. Again fate stepped into play. The night that Amanda texted me, I was on my way to pick up a pit bull puppy for my sister, Katherine.

I told Amanda to meet me the next day and I would take Ravioli to my sister's home instead of the puppy. The following day, Ravi walked into my sister's home in the beautiful North Georgia Mountains, jumped right up on the couch, and made herself right at home. She was home at last!

My sister and Ravioli are inseparable. The food aggression that Ravi had developed from starving on the streets has resolved, even when Ravi's fur-sister Indica tries to sneak a bite. Ravi's confidence in other dogs has dramatically increased.

Ravioli continues to amaze me every time I see her. Amanda started the foundation "Project Ravioli" to help raise funds for dogs such as Ravioli. We had our first fundraiser in March of 2014 where Ravioli made a guest appearance.

If Ravioli could talk, we know that she would want us to continue to raise funds for other animals like her when Amanda first found her. From the "pits" of Atlanta to the beautiful mountains of North Georgia, Ravioli has indeed touched thousands of hearts all over the WORLD.

She is not just my sister's HERO dog, but the thousands that helped her and the few that were blessed to actually know her. Thank you to all who donated to help bring this beautiful dog new joy and a new life.

UPDATE: Sadly, on October 30, 2014, Ravioli crossed the Rainbow Bridge surrounded by those who loved her. Her life was probably cut short by the abuse, neglect and malnourishment she suffered early in her life.

From her Facebook page, Project Ravioli,
https://www.facebook.com/ravioliandpuppies?fref=ts

"She had two gloriously happy years with her foster family and her new mom before she passed. Ravioli lived to know what love and compassion, family, and a full belly feel like and we will continue to strive to make sure that the same can be said for every dog.

Each and every one of you played a tremendous part in Ravi's life and we consider you all family. We can never repay the kindness that was shown to Ravioli and her puppies.

We ask that you please be respectful of the family and foster family during this time of grief.

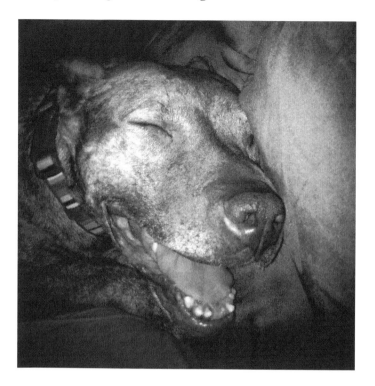

Thank you to everyone who made it possible for Ravioli to have a better life and to experience unconditional love and security. We have all been touched by this wonderful girl and, cliché though it may be, she will certainly live on in our hearts and continue to change lives through us. Rest peacefully, precious girl. You were loved."

TATORTOT (CHRISTI SMITH)

MATTIE (SARA LUNDBERG)

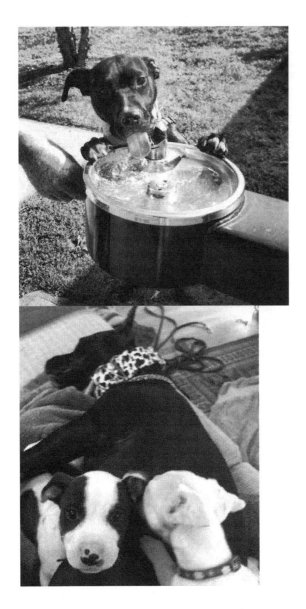

PENELOPE (ALYSSA ELLMAN)

MAJOR (UPDATE) - THANKS TO ANNA MATARESE

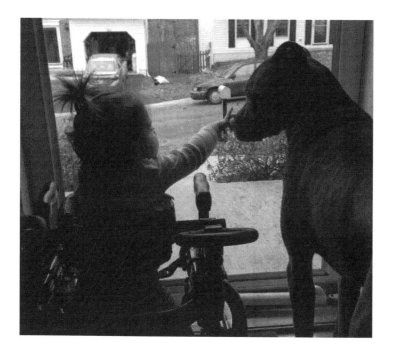

I have the best picture to share with you. Since the first book, Major has become very fond of his "baby sister." He is always by her side and looks after her. Shortly after her first birthday, Lily was diagnosed with Cerebral Palsy. This is a picture of Major helping her look out the door in her gait trainer. Best friends for life.

CHARLIE and BANDIT (BRITTANY NASH)

OLIVIA (MISTY ROSS)

PRADA (AISLINN KERN)

"When an eighty-five pound mammal licks your tears away, then tries to sit on your lap, it's hard to feel sad." Kristan Higgins

LUNA (top) and ENZO (TONI WARREN)

MONTHLY HERO RANDY – THANKS TO LORRIN TRIFILO

I remember the first time I met my boy, Randy. It was April, 2012. I was at a volunteer orientation/adoption clinic for a local pit bull rescue (Out of the Pits) and he happened to be there. I had seen his profile on the rescue's website, so I was excited to have the opportunity to meet him in person.

It was rare, if ever, that Randy got to go to adoption clinics, because he would bark and snarl uncontrollably at any dog within eyesight. On this day however, he was calm, barely paying attention to the other dogs. I said hello, spoke to his handler and knelt down to give him pats. "Oh Randy," I said to him, "if only I had a house, I would take you in a second!"

His story was a sad one, which unfortunately is all too common it seems. He was old, estimated to be between nine and twelve years old, his tail did not wag because of an old injury, his knees and elbows were calloused, the quicks in his nails were far too long from neglect, the list went on and on. He had been abandoned in New York City and left to die. One can only imagine the neglect and abuse he may have suffered in his long life before he was saved.

 Luckily, a passing dog walker had noticed him for couple of days in a row, realized that he had been abandoned and took him to a shelter. Thankfully, the staff must have seen something special in Randy and got in contact with Out of the Pits to plead his case. Knowing how difficult it is to place a senior dog, the founder of the rescue reluctantly met him, and that was it. She went in saying "I am not taking this dog," and she left saying "I could not leave this dog behind – he is too special." Randy's big, sweet, gregarious, affectionate, goofy personality saved his life. He was transported to the Albany area and brought to the vet for evaluation. There they noticed he seemed to be straining to "go." Long story short, his urethra was totally blocked by bladder stones and he needed immediate emergency surgery to save his life.

This big old pit bull, who must have been in excruciating pain, could have easily lashed out in fear and agony at any moment but he did not. Instead, he licked his caretakers and greeted them with love. This poor dog, who was probably not on the receiving end of much kindness and compassion from humans, wanted nothing more than to love and be loved by them.

Weeks and months passed. I would routinely check the rescue's website to see if Randy had been adopted, or at least placed in a foster home. Sadly, his profile was always still there. He had so many strikes against him; his age, his medical issues, including a stoma resulting from his emergency surgery that allowed him to go to the bathroom, he did not get along with cats or other dogs, so who could foster or adopt him? I could not stop thinking about him. I thought surely the chain of serendipitous events that led to saving his life occurred so he could finally have a home of his own. If anyone deserved to be spoiled and doted on it was him, but there he was, still waiting for his forever home.

It was November, 2012, and I decided to buy a home of my own.

My whole life, I had always wanted a dog, and my first thought was of Randy.

Now I could finally give him a home of his own and all the love he deserved in his golden years.

I contacted the rescue to start the process, and because Randy was everyone's favorite they were all so happy to hear that after a year and a half with the rescue, he was finally going home.

It was only a couple of weeks after moving into my house that Randy joined me and from the moment he walked in the door he made himself at home and was a perfect gentleman. For a dog that probably never lived in a house before, he had terrific manners.

Every person he met was his new best friend. He greeted every person with joy, enthusiasm and slobbery kisses, whether they wanted them or not. And just like the staff and volunteers at the rescue, everyone fell in love with him instantly. Friends and family adored him. He touched so many lives. He even earned his Canine Good Citizen Award. See – you can teach an old dog new tricks and Randy was proof. While he looked "tough" he was an ambassador for his breed and a testament to forgiveness. He was a rock star. He was truly special.

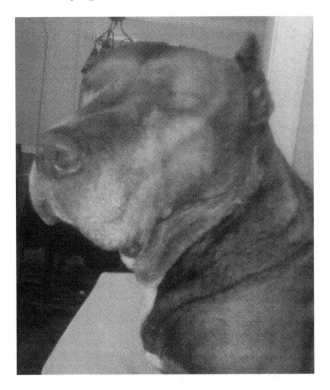

I truly believe Randy was meant to be here. If it were not for that dog walker, if it had not been for that staff person at the shelter who saw how special he was, if Out of the Pits was not able to get to him in time, if he had not had that surgery when he did, if he and I had not been at that *exact* adoption event – if even one of these things had not occurred, I would have missed out on so much.

I would have missed out on his funny quirks and the way he made me laugh, the anxious whining that would make me crazy, his waxy ears that needed daily cleaning, his goofy mannerisms and the way he would stomp around the house. I wouldn't trade any of it for anything.

Randy was with me just shy of two years, he was my first dog and taught me SO much. He was truly a gift. I was lucky to have had him. Even though our time together was short, it could not have been sweeter. Randy changed my life in so many ways. I could never begin to thank him enough for his patience while I stumbled my way through learning about being a dog owner. I miss him every day.

DOLLAR BILL (ASHLEY WRATHALL)

OUR GANG OF FOUR (BETHANN KOWALSKI)

CHLOE THE WONDER PUP – THANKS TO AMBER NEIDRAUER

Hi, I'm Chloe. My mommy calls me the wonder puppy. You might say that everyone thinks their doggie is a wonder puppy, but my mommy says no. I have defeated all odds thus far in my short life. I even have my own Facebook page and hope you enjoy following my progress and life as I grow up. Mommy has very high hopes for me and I just hope I do not disappoint her. Here is how my story begins as told by my mom:

Chloe's owners were evicted and moved away and left her mom and dad chained up with no food or shelter. A neighbor called the Sherriff's Department who called Animal Control. Sadly, the dad had already died of starvation and exposure.

The mom and puppies were emaciated and were taken to the shelter. By the next morning all the pups had died of starvation, except for Chloe.

The mom did not have milk and shelter staff does not hand feed, so she needed placement immediately. She was only a month old. To make matters worse, the Animal Cruelty Investigator could not even press charges because the officer who responded first moved the dad's body and entered the property without a search warrant.

It is easy to lose faith in humans when I hear stories like hers and I really wish her owners could have been brought to justice. The only redeeming factor was that at least Chloe had a happy ending. Not without many hurdles, though.

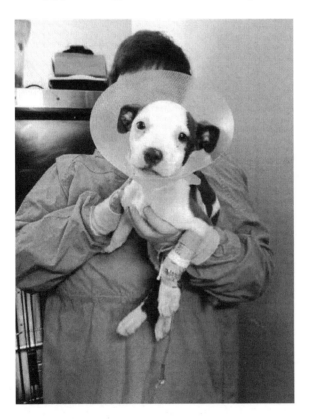

It was the power of social media that led us to Chloe. It began when my husband's nephew shared a post from a rescue called The Fort-Fortitudine Vincimus Rescue Center.

In case you are not familiar with the rescue, if you have ever seen the show *Pit Bulls and Parolees* you probably remember Jake, a regular on the show who left and started his own rescue. My husband shared the picture with me. We both immediately fell in love and filled out an application to adopt her. We did an email interview as well as a phone interview and to my surprise we were the family they chose.

The rescue is based out of North Carolina so we planned a trip to see my in-laws (who also live in North Carolina) and planned to pick her up at the same time. She was the most adorable thing we had ever seen. She even climbed up into the car seat with my infant son. Yes, she knew we were her family.

She was fine for the first two days but then started vomiting and acting lethargic. I contacted Jake and his fiancée Karin, as Karin is a vet. She told me it was critical for me to get Chloe to the vet immediately.

My in-laws put us in touch with their vet and it was confirmed that she indeed had Parvo. Once again, she fought all the odds and pulled through like a champ!

Now here in New York, she lives with us and our two kids, ages two and a half and sixteen months, her doggie brother Bowyer (a Chihuahua) and her doggie sister Miss Kitty (an Olde English Bulldog).

She is quite the character and constantly makes us laugh. Her favorite toys are water bottles, and if you are lucky she will even wait until you are finished drinking out of one before she steals it to play with it.

I hope to get her involved in therapy work at some point. She still has too much puppy in her but that is definitely a goal for the future. For now Chloe and I hope to raise awareness about the importance of spaying or neutering pets and keeping their vaccinations up to date.
https://www.facebook.com/Chloethewonderpup

MORGAN (DEBBIE McADAMS)

BLAZE (NANCY)

BELLA (BRANDY ALLEN)

MOOSE (UPDATE) - THANKS TO DANNY COMEAUX

Since Moose, the American Staffordshire Terrier and I have been off the Appalachian Trail, some very exciting things have been happening for us.

I have been off doing movies like "A Walk in the Woods," with Robert Redford and Nick Nolte which came out in August, 2015, as well as appearing in other movies and television shows.

Moose and I have added a new family member, Bryson the Prince. Bryson is a Black Labrador who showed up on my doorstep one morning a little over a year ago.

Ironically, it was the same day I received the email to do my first movie, "A Walk in the Woods." Perhaps you could say he is my lucky charm.

Even though I am mainly a pit bull guy, Bryson is now family. Moose has become a great face in the fight to end Breed Specific Legislation and helped us change laws in the city where we lived (South Bend, Indiana).

Podcasts, movies, television shows and radio shows are all on the list of things we have been off doing since our Appalachian Trail adventure.

Our incredible journey just keeps on going.

MAYA (CANDICE MUGGLIN)

MONTHLY HERO TYLER - THANKS TO SHARON MCGUIRE

When I first met Tyler he looked up into my eyes, jumped up on the bench where I was sitting, snuggled his head into my shoulder and neck and sat there calmly while I put my arms around him, held him, kissed him and talked quietly to him. He was so sweet and gentle.

The shelter volunteer told me his story and I returned a few times to walk Tyler and play fetch with him. I am of the opinion that a dog should feel safe and comfortable with a person, so I took my time and made a few visits before adopting him.

He was always happy to see me when I came to his kennel and put a leash on him. We would walk around the grounds and then go into the pen so I could throw his tennis ball over and over and over again. That was his favorite thing.

The shelter volunteer told me I could buy this dog a can of tennis balls and he would be content, but I already had a roomful of stuffed dog toys at home in the room which Tyler would soon inhabit.

After a few visits I reached the point where I could not bear to leave Tyler behind another day so I told the shelter I was going to adopt him.

Tyler had lived in two other homes before he became my dog. He was brought back to the shelter twice following divorces in his previous two homes.

Someone said to me that he was "the omen dog," but I told them I was already divorced so I was not worried.

Born in August, 2002, Tyler was at the New Rochelle Humane Society when he was a little puppy. One of the volunteers adopted him and kept him for six or seven years and, when she got divorced, returned him to the shelter.

Tyler was quickly adopted again and returned after just a few months, supposedly following another divorce. That man said he was dropping Tyler off "for a visit" and would pick him up after he ran some errands but the man never came back.

Once again, poor Tyler was homeless.

I had my own home and one room that was for the dogs I have raised over the years. The room had many stuffed animal dog toys, rawhide, tennis balls, dog puzzles, two great big L.L. Bean dog beds and a crate with a soft bed. I also had dog beds in my bedroom, the living room and the sunroom so my dogs could be comfortable everywhere.

Tyler sniffed every corner of the house and yard and made himself at home immediately. I had opened a fresh can of tennis balls for him and we played fetch in the yard and quickly became close friends.

Tyler slept on my bed at night with me until it got too warm and then he would jump down and sleep on his own bed.

My mother lived upstairs and she would babysit him when I went to work during the day. She would sit out in the backyard with him, throw his tennis ball, freshen his water and spend time with him.

They were good company for each other. Life was good.

Sad and difficult times came upon us when my mother was conned out of her life savings and had no money left. It was now up to me to pay all of the bills alone. Things became very difficult. They got even worse when my mother was diagnosed with dementia soon after and needed to go into a nursing home. Then I lost my job and went through my savings to keep the house, until eventually I too had nothing left and was forced to sell the house. I had to find a place that would take a big dog who was also a pit mix, which is how I ended up in the town where I live now.

Tyler was sad watching everything packed up in the house. Many things had to be taken away because I did not have room for everything in the new condo. I had lived for sixty-five years in the family home that my grandparents had built, but I reassured Tyler every day and spent lots of time playing with him in the backyard with his beloved tennis ball, making sure he felt happy and safe.

My next door neighbor also loved Tyler and his wonderfully sweet personality very much. She would talk to him at the fence and she would come in the evening sometimes to throw his tennis ball for him.

When the sad day came to leave our house and yard, Tyler and I had to stay in a hotel for five days until the closing on our condo. He slept up on the king-sized bed with me in the hotel room. We took walks around the area, as well as car rides.

Tyler loved to ride in the car. He would sit quietly in the back seat and look out the windows at everything around him, barking if we passed a dog and sometimes I would catch him watching me with love in his eyes.

Tyler had a hard time adjusting to condo life. He no longer had his big fenced-in backyard to run. We took long leash walks on the trails here and he enjoyed that, but we had to toss his tennis ball inside because there was nowhere to let him run outside. He was also insecure being here. It took him about three or four months before I could finally leave him alone to go to the supermarket. I was very patient with him while he made his necessary adjustment.

I found a part-time job and hired a sitter to come in to give Tyler his lunch and carrots, and take him outside. His sitter James fell madly in love with Tyler and called him "Mr. Handsome." He used to leave me notes after his visits. There was so much love in the way he spoke of Tyler, and Tyler loved him too.

Tyler had been very healthy all of his life, but at age eleven and a half he began to show symptoms of arthritis, as well as having some internal problems. His arthritis made our walks shorter and shorter as it progressed. He would fall sometimes. Other times he would go only far enough to do business and then he wanted to come back inside again.

In the warmer weather, I would take a chair and we would sit out in the grass where he would watch the birds and enjoy the sunshine. He loved to commune with nature.

Whether walking, sitting outside, or inside the house, Tyler would check in with me often. He would look up into my eyes and I would speak to him of many things and he would listen.

I loved to get down on the floor with him and hug him, pet him, talk to him and kiss him. He had a favorite music CD that he would listen to every morning. It seemed to relax him.

Whenever I put it on, Tyler would look at where the music was coming from and lie down in his place, listen to the music and close his eyes.

Tyler had many stuffed animals which he carried around, some in the living room, some in my room and some in his room.

When we came inside from a walk, he went to a rug near the front door and sat down waiting to be dried off or have his paws wiped. He did not like the cold weather, so I bought him a purple coat, and he would get excited when I picked it up to put it on him. He loved wearing his coat.

He also loved getting a bath. He would close his eyes as the warm water was poured over him and he thoroughly enjoyed being shampooed and massaged.

When he had his backyard, he would happily chase the squirrels and chipmunks around the yard. He would lie in the sunshine and watch the birds, always with his beloved tennis ball between his paws.

Tyler's health began to go downhill in early 2014. He was falling, he was sleeping more, his appetite decreased and he had little interest in walking any further than he needed to.

I took him to the vet in May, 2014 when I was seeing things that were troubling me. The vet gave him a very thorough exam and said that Tyler had lost the connection from his spinal cord to his brain. His internal organs were diseased, he had cancer throughout his entire body and after tearful discussions with his veterinarian

I made the awful decision to let him go peacefully.

Tyler left this life on May 20, 2014. His spirit remains around me. The doctor took an imprint of his paw and clipped some of his hair from around his heart. Tyler was a beautiful champagne color with a white blaze down his chest. He had an adorable lower lip that stuck out like a pout. It was endearing and everyone who noticed it smiled and said how cute he was. All of his toenails were black except for one white toenail on his hind paw. The hair around that one white nail was also white. It was an interesting marking.

There were people during his life who saw his breed and were rather hostile about it, but I always felt that Tyler had a nicer personality than those who maligned him and I told them so. He was calm, gentle and not judgmental. Tyler had a rough start in life, but when we found each other it was meant to be and we both knew it.

I told him all the time that I was so happy he was my dog. I told him every day how much I loved him. I still hold him in my heart and tell him I love him - every single day.

He was a wonderful dog and will live on in my heart forever. I only wish I had found him sooner so that I could have loved him longer.

ECHO (CAREY YARUSS SANDERS)

COLBY (MELISSA McCROHAN)

PIT BULLS I HAVE RESCUED AND ADOPTED – THANKS TO SYLVIA WHITTUM

I can remember when I feared Pit Bull Terriers and could not imagine ever owning one. That was until my daughter Sara began work as a veterinary technician at our local Humane Society in 1988.

Sara's job was difficult, as she was often asked to euthanize dogs and cats. Usually pit bulls were the first to go. Lady was our first purebred Pit Bull Terrier who had been brought in via animal control. The owner no longer wanted her and had abandoned her.

Sara just loved this small brindle baby and brought her home to my family. She was just a loving little dog who loved to follow my husband on his farm tractor as he worked around our two farms. As soon as she heard the tractor start, she would be off to be with him.

A year later, a large sixty pound male came into the shelter where Sara worked. He had been abandoned at a local convenience store and lived in the parking lot where people delighted in feeding him whatever they had on hand. He was named Rocky by the shelter employees and was a red nose with golden eyes and the biggest smile and swagger to his walk. We just had to bring him home.

He was a hit with everyone he met and a few months later he went to the local schools to become a humane education dog and ambassador for his breed. Rocky was a dog clown and at the end of each humane education class, he would start growling, howling and rolling over to the delight of the children. That was our signal that he had had enough.

During our years with Rocky we also had horses which my two girls rode and competed with at local shows and in the U.S. Pony Club. We also held fox hunts here at our farms with the Wentworth Hunt Club. I want to stress that no foxes were ever harmed here and they used a scented drag for the hunts.

There were about fifteen foxhounds that were used in these hunts. Following the events we would hold a tea and many delicious foods would be served to our guests and riders. Lady and Rocky loved these get-togethers.

One day during the start of a fox hunt, Rocky escaped from the house, to our horror. The next thing we observed was Rocky running in with the pack of hounds with a look of sheer joy and that famous pit bull grin. I do not believe he knew what he was supposed to do, but he loved the running. I am just sorry that we never thought to take a photograph. We were just so blown away with his performance.

Lady developed heart disease later in her life and died peacefully in our arms. Rocky became ill with a vascular problem and needed surgery performed as soon as possible. He died shortly after the surgery. Our hearts are still heavy from the loss of these two pit bull friends. There is not a day that we don't think of them.

Both are buried here, as are all of our other pit bulls that we later adopted.

Our next pit bull was Leroy James, who was the only one that we purchased when he was ten weeks old. We bought him from a breeder that we knew well.

Leroy was one of the last in his litter and the breeder wanted us to take him, so we did. He was the first American Kennel Club (AKC) registered Staffordshire Terrier that we had owned and was also registered with the American Dog Breeders Association and the United Kennel Club as a Pit Bull Terrier. The AKC recognized him only as an American Staffordshire Terrier.

Leroy was very large at seventy-eight pounds. He was the easiest going and most loving pup that I ever knew.

He loved everyone and especially my autistic granddaughter, whom he followed everywhere.

One time when my granddaughter was just four years old, I looked out the window to see Leroy with his jaws closed around one of her legs! In horror, I ran out and screamed at Leroy, but my granddaughter started laughing and said "Leroy has sharp teeth Nana, but he doesn't hurt me!"

That is the essence of a pit bull to me.

Leroy lived till he was 15 years old. We will never forget him.

LILY and GIGI (JENNIFER HULL)

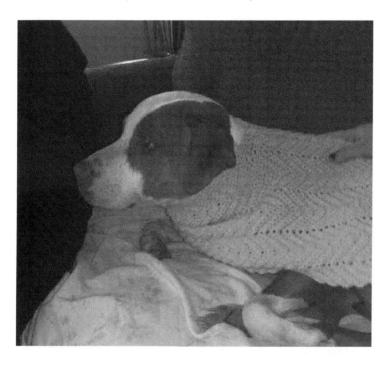

MAGNOLIA (EMILY, SMILING DOG FARMS)

SWEETPEA and FIONA (JACKIE SEAL)

MONTHLY HERO CORONA – THANKS TO JAMIE BEAM

Sixteen wonderful, rough, beautiful, amazing years. That is how long our Corona lived.

When my husband Seth was just seventeen, he was given this scared little dog by a woman he was working with. The dog was small, underweight, terrified and had a three inch scar on her right shoulder. Her name was Corona. She taught him responsibility, love, companionship and loyalty.

I came into the picture when Corona was about four and Seth and I began our lives together.

In 2008, we decided to expand our family and we got Corona a sibling, a German Shepherd/Lab mix named Bailey. He treated Corona like a mother and she allowed it. He was scared of everything and Corona was always there to protect him and keep him going.

The four of us were very happy. We went on walks around the neighborhood, day drives to explore and got a little pool that they loved to play in on nice days.

Seth and I got married and soon after, we decided to start trying for a baby. I had some difficulties and it took longer than I would have liked, but Corona was there for me through it all. Corona was the one that comforted me and let me cry.

We moved out to the country to a bigger house with a yard and lots of different smells - a happy place to raise children when and if the time came. In the meantime we decided to get another dog Dakota, a German Shepherd. Four days later we discovered we were expecting!

I knew from the start that Corona would love our baby unconditionally and that she would be the first one our child would meet when we brought him or her home. In April of 2011, our son Brayden was born.

When we brought him home, we took him straight to our bedroom and brought Corona in to meet him. Nothing against Bailey or Dakota. They were just young and had never really been around children. With Corona I knew I never had to worry. When I sat down on the bed, holding our new baby, Corona climbed up on the bed next to me. I wanted to get pictures of her meeting Brayden, so I handed him to Seth. I grabbed my camera just in time to see Corona giving Seth the gentlest kiss. It was like she was congratulating him on being a daddy and telling him that she would love and protect our son always.

She was true to her word, the most amazing dog I could have ever dreamed of for my child. When I would nurse, she was right there next to me. When he would cry, she was the first to jump up and run to him. If he fussed during a diaper change, she would lay as close as should could to try to comfort him. She would always lay right in the middle of all his toys so he had to play with her. She helped him learn to crawl by moving away from him a little at a time. When he would reach her, she would give him a kiss.

For Easter, she would wear bunny ears and be our bunny. For Christmas she wore antlers or a Santa hat. She would always dress up and let me take cute pictures of her and Brayden together. Christmas was always her favorite. She loved having a tree in the house and she loved opening presents.

In August of 2013, I made her a Facebook page, Corona the Elderbull. Her page got so much bigger than I ever expected. We started meeting many amazing people. I had no idea there were so many wonderful people in this world. Since making Corona's page, I became more and more aware of the pet overpopulation problem we have. I started seeing statistics on the amount of pit bull and pit bull type dogs that were dying every day. I started reading about Breed Specific Legislation. How did I not know all of this years ago? I learned so much, and all because of Corona.

Corona loved everyone. She was always the first to greet people who came over, she would sniff so hard it would make her sneeze. She was such a silly girl. If her fur siblings were laying in a spot on the couch that she wanted, she would bark and act like she wanted to play so they would get up. Once they got up and started trying to play with her, she would steal their spot on the couch.

Over time, Corona started showing signs of old age. She was slowing down, she took more naps, she started going off to the bedroom for alone time. We knew she would not be with us forever.

Then, in February of 2014, I saw a post on my Facebook page about a six month old pit puppy that needed a new home. Right away I started begging Seth to go get the puppy. I started sharing statistics with him and told him that we would find it a new home. I just could not handle the thought of this little puppy going to a shelter and being killed because of its breed. One less empty cage at the shelter and the chance for another dog to be adopted.

It was a forty-five minute drive to get the pup. We had no plans to keep him but when I brought the puppy named Louie out to the car, Brayden was so excited. Louie was giving him kisses and climbing all over him. Not even half way home, Seth admitted he was already attached. I just laughed at him. I knew Louie would be staying.

When Louie met Corona, he could not wait to get close to her and they began to lie together and cuddle immediately. I asked Seth if we should start trying to find him a home but he told me to wait a few days. Well, we never asked around. Louie became very attached to Corona. Brayden was completely in love. All the things that Corona was getting too old to do with him, he was beginning to do with Louie. They would run and play and go crazy together and Corona would watch with a smile.

Corona was still Brayden's number one. He always would pat her on the head and tell her she was a good girl when she took her medicine. He helps feed the dogs and he loves opening the back door for them when they need to go out. Corona was the one he always looked after though. He made sure the other dogs didn't knock her over. He always made sure she ate her food. I have pictures of him sitting on the floor with her and hand feeding her. At such a young age, Corona taught him responsibility.

I don't remember exactly when it started, I think in the spring of 2014, but Corona started having accidents in the house. She also began to show signs of confusion. With all of this though, she was still a very happy girl. She still enjoyed going outside to sunbathe. She would pick a spot in the yard, lie down, close her eyes, put her nose in the air and stay that way for as long as I would let her. She still loved to cuddle with Brayden. She still got excited and greeted daddy when he got home from work. She was eating and drinking every day. She loved getting treats and playing little games of fetch. She still had life in her and we were happy to deal with her accidents as long as her quality of life was still good. In July we celebrated her sixteenth birthday. We got her a crown, made doggy safe cupcakes, got her presents and did a little photo shoot. It was a great celebration.

In August, for my birthday, I told Seth that all I wanted was to take Corona to the beach. She had only been one time before and she loved it. Seth made it happen. She loved the car ride all the way to the beach and the walk down to the water. She played in the water for a few minutes and then laid down in the sand to enjoy the sun and breeze. I cried happy tears seeing her enjoy herself.

In October she dressed up as a ninja turtle with Brayden for Halloween. We did not take her treat or treating, but Brayden loved how cute she looked and we did a little photo shoot to show her Facebook friends.

Finally it was December - Corona's favorite time of the year. Seeing the tree made her so excited she laid right under it before we could even get it set up. She started getting cards and gifts in the mail from her friends.

Then on December 21st, she became ill and we had no idea why. She had been having trouble with her hips for a few months and now it seemed to be getting worse. She was walking slower, she had started falling down and was having trouble getting back up. There were many nights I would wake up and hear her trying to get up after she went for a drink of water and fell. We started to realize she was old, her body was shutting down and she was not going to be able to fight this and get better. She wanted to eat, she wanted to drink and she was still walking around. It was like she was fine, but her body was telling us she was not fine.

At 5 AM on Christmas Day, I was awakened by an awful, howling whine. I found Corona in the kitchen crying and unable to get up. It was then that we realized she was really suffering. We gave her a bath and when I was drying her off, she climbed into my lap and looked at me. It was that look - the one everyone tells you a dog will give you to let you know it is time. The second she looked up at me, I felt it with my whole being. I just held her and cried on the floor.

It was Christmas, Corona's favorite holiday and instead of celebrating and being happy, we were discussing letting our girl go. We decided we would make the call to her vet the next morning. We would spoil her and make her as comfortable as possible in the time we had left with her, and we would pray like crazy that just maybe she would somehow get better in the next twelve hours.

I decided she needed to spend the night in the wonderful new bed she received from her friend. After all, it was Christmas and it was her gift.

She had so many cards and gifts from her Facebook friends that she needed to open. She loved opening presents. She was so exhausted though.

Brayden sat down on the bed next to her and helped her. She stayed awake through a few gifts. I was taking pictures, but then she fell asleep. Brayden finished opening her gifts and when he was all done, he woke her up to show them to her. She sniffed them, gave her little human a thank you look and went back to sleep. The next morning I made the phone call.

The appointment was set for the next day, Saturday, December 27th at 12:30 PM. We decided to go to the store and get stuff to make her a special dinner and breakfast the next morning. Getting her to eat was not an issue.

Our sweet girl got to have one last Christmas with us, she got to sleep on the softest bed she had ever been on, she got some amazing last meals, she got to go on one last car ride and then we helped her gain her wings. My husband and I both agree that it was the hardest decision we ever had to make.

Corona was our baby. She will always be the dog that taught a man the love, loyalty, companionship and responsibility of a dog and then, years later, taught that man's son the same thing.

She will always be the one that helped me through some of my darkest days. At the time of Corona's passing, Seth and I had been trying for a second child for more than a year. I was really hoping for a daughter.

After Corona passed, I wrote her a letter. I realized how blind I had been. I had a daughter right there with me the whole time. If I never have a daughter or even another son, it is fine because I had her.

Corona is still a part of our daily lives. We have two shelves with her things set up by the window she loved to lay in front of. Brayden talks about her every single day. Rest in Peace Corona. You were and will always be our hero.

https://www.facebook.com/CoronatheElderbull

"Such short little lives our pets have to spend with us, and they spend most of it waiting for us to come home each day. It is amazing how much love and laughter they bring into our lives and even how much closer we become with each other because of them." ~ John Grogan

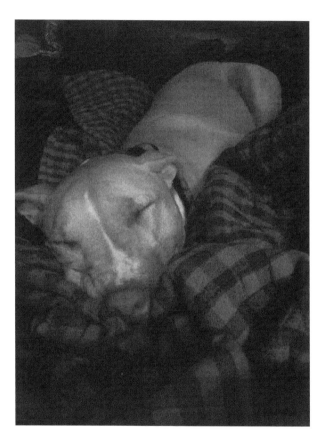

TESSA (NICOLE PIZZUTO)

DOMINIC (NEWS STORY by DAN ENGLAND)

BUDDY (HARRIET ELLS)

ALLIE (LISETTE CASTILLO)

BLUEBERRY (UPDATE) – THANKS TO MAURA PORTER

Blueberry continues with her nursing home, rehab hospital and hospice patient visits.

You can find her on Facebook

(https://www.facebook.com/pages/Blueberry-the-Pit-Bull-Therapy-Dog-Changing-Minds-One-Visit-at-a-Time/218206764888576?fref=ts)

where you will read about all of the wonderful work Blueberry does to not only change minds, but also bring joy to those who need it most.

Here are just two of the heartfelt stories shared on her page:

(March 30, 2015)

"When Blueberry arrived to visit her assigned hospice patients, we noticed we were in the 'after lunch but before Bingo' time, which means the patients are not always in their rooms but are instead moving around and can often be found in the hallways.

It is usually a great time for visits with people who are not Blueberry's 'regulars.' Today was no exception.

Blueberry met several new people who were really interested in her therapy dog work. They asked how long she had been a therapy dog, what the test was like and if she liked it.

The answer to the last one was the easiest because when she took the test, Blueberry was crawling around the rug on her belly with a huge smile on her face.

Blueberry had visited with several people when we walked by the entrance to the main common room, also known as the Bingo room. Several people were already in place with their Bingo cards, saw Blueberry and called to her. She made a grand entrance.

One woman started to sing the song 'Bingo' to her only she changed the words slightly. 'There was a farmer had a dog and Blueberry was her name-O, B-L-U-E-B-E-R-R-Y, B-L-U-E-B-E-R-R-Y and Blueberry was her name-O.'

And yes, it continued - to the end, the very end - and it was very cute.

As we neared the end of our visit time, we had still not found one of Blueberry's favorites, a woman named Ida. Ida was not in her assigned room and for a moment I thought she might have passed away, but the nurse walking by pointed us to her new room. Ida was looking tired but really perked up when she saw Blueberry and even more so when I put Blueberry up on the bed with her.

After a few minutes of lots of pets and kisses, Ida looked at me and said, 'I really love her.' I smiled at her. Then Ida added, 'I love all animals really. They are so, so – flawless.' Then I watched as she looked at Blueberry, kissed the side of her head and whispered, 'I love you' in her ear. Then a single tear slowly rolled down her cheek.

Flawless."

(July 29. 2015)

"Today at the nursing facility, we arrived just as the concert was starting. Pretty much everyone Blueberry visits was at the show, so she got to move from person to person as the music was playing. At one point the singer asked her name, and then proceeded to play 'Blueberry Hill' in her honor. The patients loved it.

A few of Blueberry's regular patients were really happy to see her in a different environment. There was even a little bit of possessiveness among the patients. 'Blueberry visits with me all the time,' I heard Mary say to the woman sitting next to her at the table who simply inquired about when Blueberry visits. Then Mary grabbed Blueberry's therapy dog vest to keep her close.

Being in a large group of patients allowed Blueberry to visit with people that she normally does not visit. As we walked amongst the crowded tables, I watched hands drop down for brush touches as she passed. A few people motioned her over. One woman we had not met before kept looking at Blueberry wide-eyed. After a minute or so of her gently touching Blueberry's head and ears, she looked at me with tears welled in her eyes and said, 'I just love dogs.'

Just a handful of patients were not at the concert, but we set out to find them in their rooms. It was an indication that they were feeling too low to attend. Every one of them was sleeping. They all looked too comfortable to wake. As we were leaving one room though, I noticed the patient was awake now and she was waving at Blueberry. I stopped Blueberry and turned her so she was facing the woman. The woman kept looking at Blueberry and then mouthed the word 'bye.' I had to wonder if it was a final goodbye.

It would be fitting and most appropriate for the goodbye to go to a dog. There are so many humans in these facilities, but dogs - well there are not enough of them, and each visit with a dog is a way to bring a smile and a happy memory. 'I just love dogs.' Peace all."

MIDNIGHT (KAYDINCE DUPRE)

EDDIE JUSTICE (CLAUDIA STAUBER)

VICTOR - MOM LINDA, MAKING OF MIRACLES STORIES (MOMS) RESCUE, CARAPATHIA PAWS AND ONE STEP CLOSER ANIMAL RESCUE (OSCAR)

DEMON (AMELIA RODRIGUEZ)

"Pit Bulls are famous, in circles of knowledgeable dog people, for the love and loyalty they bestow on anyone who shows them a smidgen of kindness." ~ Linda Wilson-Fuoco

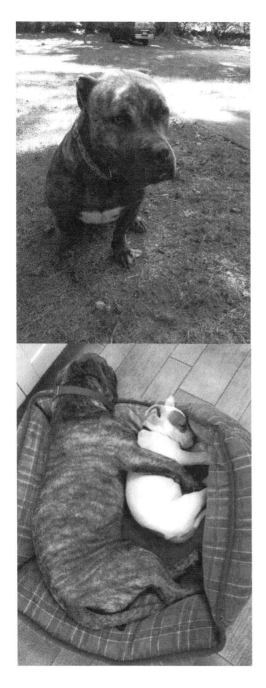

FLASH and STELLA (BETSY FURST)

MONTHLY HERO PETEY – THANKS TO STACY BOVE-FULGENZI

I have quite the pack at home. My fur kids are two Boxers, one American Staffordshire Terrier Blue Nose, one American Staffordshire/Hound Mix that we are fostering and my American Pit Bull Terrier, Petey who, as you will see, is my hero!

Petey came into my life in December of 2010. I had just lost the oldest of my four pups, Nikki, and was truly heartbroken. It was around this same time that a friend had a young male American Pit Bull Terrier that he was looking to place in a loving home.

I was just not ready to adopt another dog as my heart had not even begun to mend over our recent loss, so I pushed it off. Then the day came that I went to my friend's home with my husband to give advice on an unrelated matter. That was the day I met this sweet little guy, and knew in a heartbeat that Nikki would have loved him. On top of that, my husband who didn't want even one dog, let alone four, turned to me and said, "We are not leaving without Petey." I looked at him and said, "I guess not, since you have already named him." It seemed it was meant to be - Petey adopted us that day.

Petey was only about five months old when we took him home, and I guess you could say his personality reminded me a lot of Nikki's, only the male version of course. He was now the baby in our pack, and I believe he helped not only my husband and me, but also my other pups to get through the loss of Mama Nikki, who looked out for us all. Now we all needed to put our focus on taking care of the new canine kid in the family.

The dogs all get along beautifully, even though each one has a different personality and all are different breeds. People must understand that with all dogs, no matter what the breed, boundaries need to be set, just like you would with children. So in essence, your children can be polite or impolite, sweet or fresh, depending on how they are raised. And, like children, dogs need to know what is expected of them.

I have four dogs of my own and one foster for a total of five. They all eat in the same room without attempting to go for each other's food bowls. I believe in time out, and positive reinforcement. I am no expert, but I carry such a love and passion for my pups and this seems to work in our home. In addition, it helps that they are all quite the cuddle bugs.

Petey started going to classes introduced to me by a dear friend, and he loved it. He thrived on being involved, and being around others, so we just kept going and started taking classes for the Canine Good Citizen (CGC), and Pet Therapy Training Programs.

Petey was tested by Therapy Dog International (TDI) and passed with flying colors. Amazing how it was Petey who always made me look good as a trainer. Believe me when I say he deserves all the credit!

Now I consider my four-year-old American Pit Bull Terrier, Petey, to be a HERO. This is not something we should take for granted, but this is certainly typical of this breed.

Petey is a Therapy Dog that LOVES his work, and looks forward to visiting one of New York's top hospitals. He also attends many events, including the New York Rangers Dog Walk and even met Head Coach John Tortorella!

Petey's mission has been to help others, provide a bit of relief to some, and place some smiles on the faces of others. And that is what he does, for patients and staff alike.

I cannot count the number of times I have been stopped by hospital employees when they spot Petey on his way in or out of the hospital for visits. They kneel down to pet him, hug him or give him his favorite belly scratches.

I can't count the number of times I have heard, "I needed to see Petey today, he is my therapy," or "Petey is here, I'll have a better day now."

I am blessed with sweet Petey. I am happy to share him with anyone who needs a friend. He is loved by everyone he meets and brings joy into the lives of those who need it the most. And that is why Petey is my HERO!!

BENTLEY (JEFF STATHAM)

8BALL (RACHEL LEE)

"You can say any foolish thing to a dog, and the dog will give you a look that says, 'Wow, you're right! I never would've thought of that!'" Dave Barry

KOOL-AID (KATHI WHEELER)

ROCCO, DOZER and CLARENCE (DANA JONES)

MILLIE (UPDATE) - THANKS TO KATIE ELLIS

Millie is now a Certified Therapy Dog! Every Saturday we visit a local nursing home. All of the residents love her. She is as sweet as can be and looks forward to going to the nursing

home and doing what she does best – bringing smiles to the faces of everyone she meets.

Millie and I are working hard to help people to see how wonderful this breed really is. It is amazing how far she has come. When we adopted her she was so skinny and scared but now you would have no idea how bad the first five years of her life were. She was overbred and had to have a lot of teeth pulled because she was most likely kept in a cage and tried to chew her way out.

Millie is proof that pit bulls are amazing and we as humans can learn a lot from them. They may be the underdog to some, but those who know them know better. They can move on with their lives and not think about the past. What a great lesson for all of us.

Millie now has three brothers, Brody (a Boxer), Bently (a Husky mix) and Linus (a pit bull/Boxer mix) and a pit bull sister named Lucy. Lucy and Linus were both found in our neighborhood and no one claimed them so they joined our pack. Our house is a crazy house but I would not want it any other way!

Please follow Sillie Millie on Facebook for all of her latest adventures.
https://www.facebook.com/SillieMillie1?fref=ts

SEAMUS (CORRI JIMINEZ)

KANE AND TESS (KANE'S KRUSADE)

MAC – THANKS TO KATE BASTIDA

I grew up with dogs – Boxers that my dad would bring home as puppies. So I knew, when I moved away to California ten years ago, that it would only be a matter of time until I had a dog of my own. I decided to rescue but still was not considering any breed other than a Boxer. The problem was, I could not get any dog. Every time the inkling came up or I brought it up with my mother (who was helping support me on and off as I was still in school) she became furious with me.

She said it was "nervy" to even consider such a time and money-consuming investment when I was not financially independent yet. She was right, plus she always added that I should wait until I had a big enough place, preferably with a yard, if I was going to get a big dog. I figured I would have to wait until I was married, so I could share the responsibility of pet care and hopefully have enough space.

Marriage was nowhere in sight though. I was perpetually in dead-end situations with guys. I would either get involved with someone I had no real attachment to, or I would run away frightened if I thought my feelings would be hurt. I had already lost plenty and hurt a lot, but I refused to let it show – the last thing I wanted was to appear needy.

When I opened an email my friend Sarah sent me on June 10, 2012, I expected it to be like several others she had forwarded me over the years; dog rescue listings with cute pictures and/or sob stories about whatever breed it was that needed a home.

Sarah is one of the kindest people I know, a hybrid Mother Teresa meets Daddy Warbucks. She was not able to adopt any more dogs because she already had two that did not care for most other dogs, but she had always told me if I ever wanted to adopt a dog she would help me with the cost. As generous as Sarah's offer was, I never truly considered it. I barely feel comfortable letting a friend buy me coffee, much less pay for the costs a pet would incur.

That night though, she forwarded me the email about Mac. Something told me this was different. I actually wanted to take her up on her offer. That was the first lesson I learned from Mac, and it was before I had even met him. He taught me to ask for and be able to accept help.

To this day, I am not sure what drew me to Mac. The video portrayed him as loving and desperate for a home, but I had seen plenty of dog rescue ads like that. He was not a Boxer pup – he was a seven year old American Staffordshire/Mastiff mix – and I did not even find him that cute to begin with. It seems silly now because I get so many compliments on how good-looking he is.

I laugh to myself as I remember thinking I was going to have to accept that I would just have one of those "ugly dogs." The conditions of his health, his stature, size and breed did not make him any more appealing.

It was only about halfway into the YouTube video (approximately two minutes in) that my heart melted and I was stuck. I watched him get a bath at the shelter. I looked at this filthy animal as he, with so much relief, leaned in to the shelter employee who was washing him. I had never witnessed so much gratitude, kindness and compassion all at once. I had to meet him.

Over the next 48 hours, I researched everything possible on pit bulls. I talked to as many dog (and pit) owners as I could. I went to every website and read every piece of literature out there.

I filled pages of a yellow notepad with "Things to Consider," followed by every reason I could think of to not get the dog and/or ways he would complicate and change my life forever.

I am anything but impulsive, so this was not a decision I was just going to jump into. But with Sarah pushing me to at least go visit Mac, I figured I should at least check him out in person at the vet's office where he was staying.

There was no pressure from the rescue group (Angel City Pit Bulls) either, as they seemed to be giving me the brush-off in favor of a family who must have seemed more suitable.

I went to meet Mac knowing it was simply a first date, with no promises or strings attached…yet.

It seems like everyone I knew who had rescued a pet had the "I saw him and he looked at me and I just knew" moment. Since my only experience was with breeders – where my dad pointed out which was the best pup to take home – I had never experienced the instant love affair I had heard my friends describe in rescuing or adopting a dog. But I imagined, much like falling in love for the first time or meeting my future husband, that it would hit me like a bolt of lightning, and that I'd know once I felt it.

So on Tuesday, June 12, 2012, I walked in to meet Mac thinking two things:

1. If Mac was the dog for me, I would know immediately when I saw him, and
2. If it was not meant to be, the other family would be chosen.

Out came this 90-pound, snorting, sniffling, grunting beast into the small room where I was waiting. We were then left alone in the room to get acquainted. Mac stared at the closed door without even acknowledging that I was in there with him.

It reminded me of a scene in the movies where a prisoner is tossed into a cell but is so focused on the fact that he is behind bars that he does not even notice that someone is in there with him.

I hesitated, scared to start petting him since he did not seem that interested in getting to know me. Extending my arm out, I slowly rubbed his back – as far away from his face as I could get while still touching him. He continued to ignore me for what probably was only ten or fifteen seconds but felt like a half hour.

"I guess this is it," I thought, "I mean he won't even look at me, and I don't really feel any sort of connection to this animal at all." Needless to say, it definitely was not the romantic first encounter I had been expecting.

I sighed – with relief and a bit of disappointment. I was about to chalk up the experience to my being a sap and falling for a well-made YouTube video. Then, in that minute, right before I stood up to get my purse, Mac turned around and walked up to me – his face right in mine – and, as if to tell me I passed the test, began covering my face with kisses.

I melted into tears, as he proceeded to walk circles around me kissing every bit of skin he could. Ironically, he has never kissed me or anyone like that again since that day – totally not his style to cover people in kisses. I guess he just knew this time was an exception. It was his way of ensuring the "I just knew" moment would happen for me, as I had hoped.

The "Things to Consider" list was tossed in a drawer that afternoon and the only thing I was worried about now was *not* getting the dog at this point. Angel City Pit Bulls was not returning my calls or giving me any real answers so I began to resolve myself to the "maybe it's not meant to be" idea again.

I had promised Mac that no matter what, I would see him again, even if it was just for a friendly visit at the ICU, since the vet said he was not getting many visitors. So a few days later I went back to see him.

They put me in a room with a couch and this time a whole new dog entered the room. It was like he recognized me and could not believe I had come back.

As I sat on the couch just observing him in his new-found spirit. Mac crawled up on the couch next to me to just sit there together. I videotaped the climb up (it did not look easy for him) and later found out that it was the first time he had ever done that.

Had we become best friends?

Mac helped me make another decision that day – it was to take the plunge with this new relationship, even with all the changes it was going to mean, some harder than others.

I knew that my new role as a pet parent would definitely impact my job as a drug and alcohol counselor at a non-profit rehab facility.

It would certainly affect my schedule – now I would need to drive home for lunch each day to take Mac out for a walk.

Also, friends joked that I was adopting this "project" dog to fulfill my own codependent needs; to be a caregiver.

I wondered, would the emotionally-taxing days of working with needy people make it harder to come home to a special needs dog, or more rewarding?

What I did not think of, in all of my speculation, was the impact that having Mac in my life would have *on* my work.

That is, what he would teach me about being a professional helper – and what *he* would do for the community – how he would leave his pawprint on the hearts of some of the residents more than I ever could.

This photo, in which Mac is wearing a blue "adopt me" bandana, may be the first picture we ever took together.

That was the day three years ago when I met him, after Angel City Pit Bulls took him out of the shelter in such poor condition that he needed to be quarantined at the vet.

That was the day my life changed forever.

Mac and I enjoy taking road trips together.

Recently we have actually taken a big one – moving across the country to live in North Carolina with my brother, my seven year old nephew and their pit puppy Cookie, who may be Mac's biggest fan.

I can't wait to see what adventures lie ahead for me and my sweet pibble Mac.

GENTLE GIANTS (NATASHA THOMPSON)

CHEYENNE (VALERIE WOOLEY)

SAMANTHA (DAWNMARIE SOUZA)

MONTHLY HERO NALA – THANKS TO STEVE FONTANELLA

One day as I was in the parking lot at my vet's office, after making the tough decision to put my best friend of twelve years down due to very aggressive cancer, my phone rang.

I'm not sure why I answered it but I did. It was a friend of mine from the Hartford, Connecticut Police Department. He was telling me about a very nice stray dog that had been picked up.

He really hoped I could help.

Again, I was in the parking lot of my vet trying to get the courage to go inside with Sheba. I basically told him to go away and thanks for thinking of me.

A few days later, I was looking at the City of Hartford Facebook page and saw her for the first time. Something told me she was the one.

I thought it was too soon to bring another dog into our home, but I knew she needed me.

I called Sherry, the Animal Control Officer, and said I would like to see Prada, #477. I asked about the sores on her legs and she was surprised I saw them in the pictures.

We went to meet Prada and it was love at first sight.

She weighed only twenty-one pounds at the time. She now weighs fifty-four.

After introducing her to our other rescue Miley, a Lab/Border Collie mix, and laying some ground rules, she seemed to fit in nicely.

Her new name is Nala (Lion King reference for the kids) and she has quickly become an advocate for pit bulls everywhere.

She would frequent the assisted living facility where my grandmother and my wife's grandmother lived. She allowed the residents to pet her and they let us talk to them and educate them about the pit bull breed.

She connected us with the AMAZING ladies from Kenway's Cause, a foundation set up to help the animals of Hartford, with whom we have quickly become very close friends.

Nala has inspired us to run fundraisers in the form of golf events, dinner dances and comedy shows to raise money to help pups in need. Literally tens of thousands of dollars have been raised to help Kenway's Cause, and all because of Nala.

When people have questions or negative ideas of what a pit bull is, I introduce them to Nala. She, on her own, changes minds almost immediately.

Most importantly, she has led us to begin fostering dogs in need. In 2014, we fostered four pits.

Nala helped train one of the pups that had aggression issues. Two others had parvo. Nala knew to be gentle with them and then taught them how to play when they were ready.

Lastly, we fostered a pit puppy who had been pulled out of a house during a police raid. Nala also sets the mood with all three of our rescues when a foster comes into the house. She is the only one that plays outside with them at their pace. When anyone in our family is ill she insists on sleeping on or near them to make sure they are alright.

She has even gone so far, on two separate occasions, to stop me from stepping on a copperhead snake in the backyard. She rides on my lap when I mow the lawn and is by far the most intelligent, loyal and inspiring little dog I have ever met in my life.

She currently lives in a house with me, my wife Jen and two young daughters, Madison (age ten) and Ashley (age three) and Miley, the Lab/Border Collie mix, Chloe a pit mix who was severely abused, and a foster, Emma, who is a pit/Plott Hound mix. Yes ALL females.

Whenever I have a bad day I come home and go straight for Nala. She always knows how to make us feel better.

It is hard to think that what we do is out of the ordinary. We love dogs. We love Kenway's Cause and we LOVE everyone involved with helping these AMAZING animals. Without Nala I would not have met the ladies from Kenway's Cause and our lives would be very different today.

Nala is our HERO!

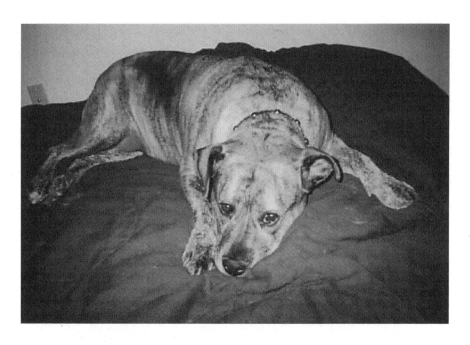

MYSTIQUE (DEAN FIORA)

CESAR, MR. BOLT and HOPE (MARY and SCOTT LAMBERT)

RUFUS (MARIE BRIGGS)

"Never slow down, never look back, live each day with adolescent verve and spunk and curiosity and playfulness. If you think you're still a young pup, then maybe you are, no matter what the calendar says." ~ John Grogan

HUDSON (RICHARD NASH)

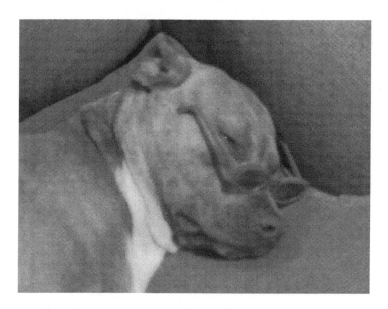

PHOENIX (KIMBERLY BANKS

KYRA (UPDATE) – THANKS TO LEA ERVIN

Kyra is now seven years old and she is doing great. She has had both of her ACLs rebuilt, about a year apart, but gets around pretty well for a "senior" dog. She is beginning to get a little gray in her snout though. I tell her we are just a couple of middle-aged ladies.

Kyra is continuing to change people's minds about pit bulls. She is an excellent ambassador for the breed.

She loves kids and kids love her. It is beautiful to watch when we are out walking in the park and we come upon a child. It does not matter how big or how old, Kyra's eyes light up and she wants to go give kisses. Some of the kids' faces just light up when they see her. We then spend several minutes letting them play and love each other.

Sometimes there is a child that seems intimidated, probably because of her size, or because the parent is hesitant because of Kyra's breed. Kyra always seems to know to be extra gentle with these kids. I cannot count how many times parents have told us that Kyra is the first big dog their children have petted. It is a pure joy to watch this happen, as each new child becomes more comfortable Kyra will move closer and give them gentle kisses.

Kyra also loves older folks. My parents are a perfect example. I have seen Kyra play tug with my mother (now in her seventies) and Kyra is much gentler with her than when she is playing with my son who is in his twenties. It is amazing what a good judge she is. She just seems to know how hard she can pull, play, or jump.

Not much else has changed, except perhaps me. I can honestly say that Kyra has made me a much better person. I am so very fortunate to have her in my life. She has taught me about loyalty, unconditional love, patience, and just enjoying being alive.

Kyra saved me!

DIAMOND, ZOEY and NATAS (JAMIE HARRIS)

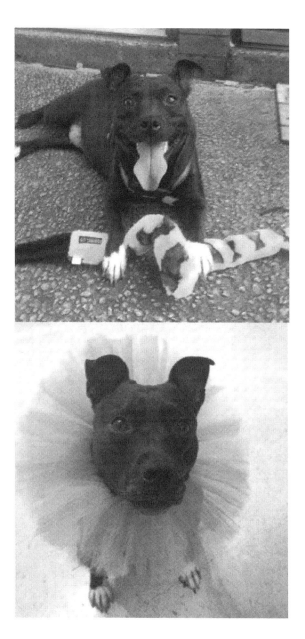

MISS PIGGY (ANNE DOBNAK)

ROSIE and KENNA

DIESEL

MAX
ROSIE, KENNA, DIESEL and MAX (LAUREN LEE)

MAC (ROCHELLE STEFFEN)

MONTHLY HERO NESSA -THANKS TO PAM SIMONS

My husband and I have an almost three-year-old pittie pup. We originally got her for my young adult nephew who was living with us and going through a difficult time in his life. He needed something positive to focus on, so we agreed that having a dog would be good for him. He had his heart set on getting a pit bull, because a few of his friends had them, but my husband and I were hesitant because we heard they were vicious dogs and we believed it.

I began doing research on the breed and finally gave in. My nephew began his search for the perfect dog. Our only stipulation was that whichever dog he chose had to be good with cats and of course other dogs since we had both a cat and a five-year-old Lab.

We live a small community and at the time there were not many pit bull type dogs available, so we broadened our search to Las Vegas.

We looked for different pet adoption events and came across a few dogs we wanted to see. One of the events advertised two female pit bull puppies, about twelve weeks old that had been found in a garbage dumpster.

Seriously, who does that?

Anyway, by the time we arrived at the location, one of the puppies had already been adopted. We hung out with the other puppy for a bit and she immediately stole my heart. She was adorable and a snuggle-bug, so we made the decision to adopt her.

Although she would be my nephew's dog, I was already in love with her. She needed to be spayed, so it was a week before we were actually able to bring her home. My nephew named her "Nessa."

I tried my best not to get too attached to her since she was not technically mine, but I did want her to get into a routine, so we began feeding and walking her with our Lab. Our dog and cat adjusted well to Nessa. Everything was great. I was in love with her but as difficult as it was, I kept my distance.

Sadly, even Nessa could not help when my nephew fell back into drugs and was sent to prison. Now my husband and I were responsible for this sweet pup while he was gone. My nephew decided that since he would be away for two years, it would be better if we just kept her. Honestly, I was happy with his decision. I couldn't bear the idea of parting with her.

Nessa is the reason our view of pit bulls has changed. She is the most lovable, snuggly, smart, happy dog I have ever seen. She has definitely made us more active. While my Lab is content with walking in the neighborhood, with Nessa we do more. We are out with her every week, exploring the many local hiking trails in our area. Her favorite thing to do is to find the perfect stick, not just for fetching but to carry in her mouth when we are out on a trail. She is very proud of her sticks and has quite the collection in our yard. If you have an Instagram account, look up #stickoftheday and you will see many pictures of her.

We have gone from being among those who feared pit bulls because of the way they are portrayed in the media to being advocates for the breed and all because of Nessa. This sweet little puppy, who had been thrown away like trash, has grown into a beloved member of our family. Now we cannot imagine our lives without her. She has overcome horrific beginnings, opened our hearts and changed, not only our minds but also many others. And that is why Nessa is our hero!

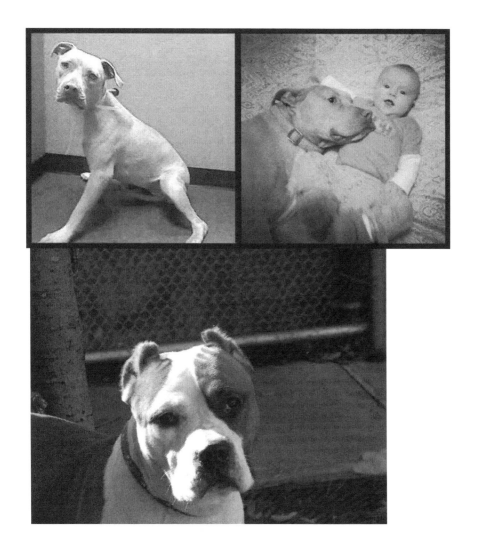

JADE and MANNY (ELISA LAFONT)

STELLA (PAULA DILLON)

COCO and SOPHIE (JOYCE STEVENSON)

WALTER (UPDATE) - THANKS TO LYNN READY

Back in January, 2015, Walter's mom Lynn wrote: "Walter is still happy as ever and in fact, he has started laser therapy and acupuncture and it is really helping his arthritis!"

Sadly, in August, 2015, Walter earned his wings. Posted on his Facebook page August 29, 2015: "Hey friends I am writing to tell you that I am in Heaven now. I had a rough past few days and nights and while Mom and Dad tried everything, Dr. Ruffing thought I might have either had a mini stroke or the lymphoma spread to my brain because I just couldn't get comfortable and I was running into everything. I was very uncomfortable and I think it was hard to watch. But guess what - I got to see my sister Livi here! And I saw GG and Nola and I met a lot of wonderful new friends like Molly, Max, Baxter, Gracie and Roxy. It is nice not being in pain anymore. It is nice being at peace. I am glad Mom and Dad cared enough about me to let me be at peace and not keep me around for themselves.

I was a fighter and battled so many illnesses in the past few months. Today they gave me the kindest gift they could have given me. Thank you all for caring about me. Mom will never forget the day she brought me home to live my new life in my wonderful home where I had four amazing years."

Walter will be remembered by so many. He was a Therapy Dog and an amazing ambassador. His mom will continue his Facebook page in his memory.
https://www.facebook.com/walter.ready.5

SKYE (MICHELLE CULHANE)

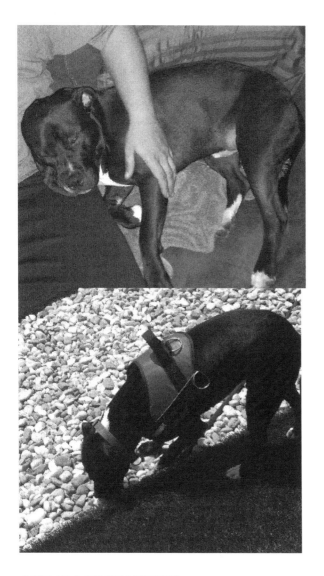

ABRAM (ELIZABETH)

DUCHESS (REBECCA MORLEY)

"A dog has no use for fancy cars, big homes, or designer clothes. A water logged stick will do just fine. A dog doesn't care if you're rich or poor, clever or dull, smart or dumb. Give him your heart and he'll give you his. How many people can you say that about? How many people can make you feel rare and pure and special? How many people can make you feel extraordinary?" ~ John Grogan

MONTHLY HERO KIYOSHI - THANKS TO TARA BROUSSEAU

Today I will share with you the story of love and loss and how my life changed forever, the instant I met him.

Eleven years ago I was honored to be chosen as the new Mama to a pit mix who was saved from a high kill shelter in Virginia. A woman from New England made one or two trips a month to save urgent dogs from kill shelters down south. Most of these dogs were hound dogs. However, on this particular day she came across a dog who had one day left before being euthanized. She said his eyes were so sad there was no way she could leave him.

He had a story to tell. I came across him on a pet adoption site and inquired immediately.

His story was one of the most horrific and heart wrenching I had ever heard. He was at least five years old and had endured an abusive, neglectful and lonely existence. His "people" had tied him to a three foot lead outside with no food or water and admitted to trying to starve him to death so they didn't have to surrender him to a shelter and pay the one dollar fee.

When he arrived at my home, he would not eat or drink. He would not walk up or down the stairs to get outside. He had bad cataracts and broken teeth, probably from eating rocks or anything he could get within reach. I carried him everywhere, I hand fed him and in time he began to trust me.

He would not leave my side and often looked sad. It broke my heart over and over but I tried to remain positive, for I was giving him a new life, and he embraced the opportunity and made the most of it.

He loved everyone and every animal he ever met. He carried a tennis ball everywhere he went and fell asleep with one in his mouth every night. He was my gentle bear, so I gave him the name "Kiyoshi."

Sadly, five and a half years ago, at about age ten or eleven, he crossed the bridge. It was as if my soul had left my body. I was distraught and lost.

I still do not go one day without crying and asking why he had to leave. I believe however, that he was really the one who saved me because for the first time in my life, my heart was full when I was with him.

Thank you Kiyoshi. I am so sorry for what those people did to you. We will be together again someday.

Here is my poem to you:

On this day five years ago
The Rainbow Bridge you crossed
And each day since I sit in silence
Suffering...so lost
Your first contact with whom you thought
Would keep you safe and warm
Betrayed your trust, neglected you
Abused and did you harmHow lucky was I to be the one
To give you a second chance
Your body frail, eyes nearly blind
Though I loved you at first glance

With arms open wide I carried you
Wherever you needed to go
Sipping water from my hands, sleeping in my arms
As your trust began to grow
I named you Kiyoshi, for you were just that
My beautiful 'gentle bear'
No hate in your heart but love so contagious
Everyday was a breath of fresh air
You redefined peace, forever so loyal
Your love had known no bounds
Your sweet gentle eyes and soft brown fur
How I've longed to hear the sounds
Of your joy and elation as I'd walk through the door
Soft whimpers and sighs of relief
That I'd come back to you each day and the next
Forever was what I believed
That just wasn't so, five years had flown by
Please give me just one day more
To hold you and love you and tell you how much
Your beauty I truly adore
I only hope I gave you the life
You deserved and that you should know
With each passing day, my heart cries for you
Yet my love still continues to grow
The next time we meet, we will never part
Near a bridge without any cares
So until then you'll fly free in my soul
My Kiyoshi..my Gentle Bear

****

After I lost Kiyoshi, I was so unbelievably filled with sorrow, the only thing I felt I could do was rescue another in his memory.

Two weeks later I adopted my beloved boy who came from a kill shelter in New York City. I believe Kiyoshi sent him to me. I named him Kikoda, koda meaning friend in Dakota Indian.

In May of 2013, I adopted a female pit who was taken from her mother at two weeks old and was being sold on Craig's List before a rescue group got her.

I have since become close friends with her foster mom, who cared for her until she was five months, when I adopted her. I named her Soleil, and in August, 2014, I rescued a pittie puppy who, with his littermates, was seized by Animal Control in a cruelty/neglect case. Two of his siblings did not make it. He is still being treated for mange and had the worst case of worms I have even seen. I named him Kinkade.

OLIVIA (LYNN TELLER)

LUCKY (STACY HALLMAN)

"The two most important days in your life are the day you are born and the day you find out why." ~ Mark Twain

TYE (ERICA KUTZING)

Erica continues to take in special needs animals and hospice cases. She is truly an angel to those who are most in need.

LILLY THE HERO PIT BULL (DAVID LANTEIGNE)

MACIE (BRITTNIE)

BRUNO - THANKS TO SHANNON GRAHAM

It is amazing how one image can change your life. I find it hard to believe, and yet that is exactly what happened to me. On a typical day in December, 2014, I was scrolling through my Facebook newsfeed. I do this several times each day to break up the day and fight boredom. Being actively involved in animal rescue, I have a lot of friends that share my passion. I am used to seeing images of dogs that are in need of rescue or foster. I see their faces, shake my head, say a little prayer and scroll down. That is a sad thing to get used to; images of dogs that are starved, abandoned, sad, unwanted and unloved.

However, on this particular typical day as I was scrolling down, I was caught by an image, or rather a collage of images in one. I believe that it was the way that he leaned his head into the volunteer, so trusting and thankful that made me stop on this picture. I wanted to know more. I read the attached post that explained that the dog in the collage was named Bruno.

Bruno was left tied to a pole on the side of the street in Brooklyn, New York and waited two days for Animal Care and Control to pick him up and take him to an extremely high kill shelter. To make matters worse, Bruno is blind, Bruno is old, and Bruno is a pit bull. This is typically a death sentence for dogs like Bruno. No one wants an old, blind dog, much less an old, blind pit bull. Except someone did want Bruno; I did!

I took a look at that picture for a good five minutes. Then I shook my head, said a little prayer and kept scrolling. Then I went back to his picture again and again until I finally decided that I had enough of looking. I made up my mind. I called the president of the rescue that I foster for and said that although I was supposed to be on a break from fostering due to a hectic work, school and family schedule, I would do whatever it took to bring Bruno to our home and foster him.

Thankfully, I have gained the reputation of being a reliable foster, and volunteer within our organization so when I say I want a dog, if it is not already spoken for, I usually get it, for better or worse. Coincidentally, the president had just sent an email for more information on Bruno. This was a good sign! Transport was arranged to bring Bruno to upstate New York from Brooklyn within a week.

Panic suddenly set in. I had no idea how to properly care for a blind dog. From that moment, I started scouring the internet for as much information as possible on how to care for a blind dog. He was coming and I felt totally unprepared. Some of the things that I learned online included; covering any sharp edges in my house, helping him to mentally map out the house, and creating a safe zone for him in case he got disoriented. I decided that his safe place would be his crate. I put a nice cozy bed in there for him along with some toys and bones. I also found items online to help blind dogs have a more comfortable, quality life. I found the Jenny leash (a very short leash used more as a lead to keep the dog close to you), the Halo (a harness with a guard that extends around the dog's face to protect him from bumping into things), and Jolly balls that smell like oranges and blueberries so the dog can smell the ball rather than see it. I felt that with the knowledge I gained through my research I would be better equipped to make a good, safe environment for Bruno.

The day finally arrived when Bruno came home. The minute I saw him, all the confidence that I had went out the window. He not only bumped into everything, he could not see there were steps, so he would fumble and trip over any little change in the terrain in which he was walking. That first week I wondered if I had what it took to make sure that Bruno was safe and happy. On the one hand, I was filled with self-doubt. On the other hand, I knew that the care that my family and I were providing was a lot better than what he had prior to coming to us. We would never abandon him. We would never leave him feeling confused and scared. As long as we had breath in our bodies, he would always have a home.

Another thing I was not prepared for with Bruno was just how amazing he is. He is the most loving, happy, cuddly, mush man ever! He is a goof ball. He loves every single person he meets. He is not fazed by other animals and happily greets them with a butt sniff and a tail wag.

Bruno is the type of dog that will steal your heart with one glance. He does not hold a grudge and is filled with so much love for the human race. He does not discriminate. As long as you are willing to give him some affection, he will take it. He is a true ambassador for his breed.

Almost exactly one month after getting Bruno, our family made the decision to make him a permanent part of our family. This decision was made with a lot of thought and care. Selfishly, we wanted to adopt him, but we also know that as a foster family, we always make the decision that is best for the dog. We were blessed to be what was best for Bruno. It wouldn't be fair to him to have to get acclimated to another new environment. He is happy in our home. He is loved. He is spoiled!

Every single day I ask Bruno, usually as I am hugging and kissing him, how I got so lucky to have him as my dog. I truly do not think the people that left him knew just what they were leaving tied to a pole on that cold December day. If they had an ounce of recognition for Bruno's true soul, there is no way that they ever would have left him.

While I love all my dogs very much, I have never had a dog like Bruno before. He embodies everything that is good and right. He makes me want to be a better person; to be more loving, and forgiving, to live in the moment and not take anything for granted and to be silly and goofy.

I do not know how long I have with Bruno but I will forever be thankful that he was brought into my life.

JAKE MENTORS FOSTERS KADIN and ODIE (BRENDA PANE)

MARLEY

MARLEY CONT'D (BONNIE DICOCCO)

PIPER (UPDATE) – THANKS TO LAURA BRUCCOLERI

Piper continues to bring joy to autistic children by visiting them at their schools and camps. She also mentors dogs and puppies in training.

This past summer, Piper also hosted summer classes in her home state of Indiana to help other dogs learn proper manners and teach dog safety to their owners.

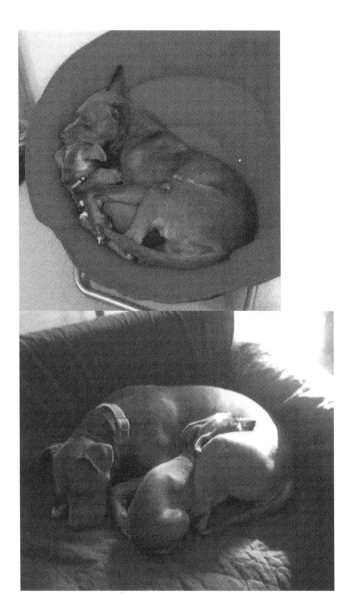

ROXIE (CHRISTINA CUEVAS)

"A dog is not a thing. A thing is replaceable. A dog is not. A thing is disposable. A dog is not. A thing doesn't have a heart. A dog's heart is bigger than any 'thing' you can ever own." ~ Elizabeth Parker

PUMA – R.I.P. October 2014 (JACQUELINE DRAKE)

KAYLA (JEANIE SCHULZ)

GULLIVER (JEANIE CHRISTENBURY)

MONTHLY HERO SULLIVAN – THANKS TO CHRISTINE COLLINS

I always knew I wanted to rescue a pit bull or pit bull mix, and one day while perusing PetFinder, this adorable face showed up.

There was something about this boy that made me drive three hours to New Hampshire from my home in Maine to meet him. It was love at first sight. He was loving, gentle, playful and the cutest thing I had ever seen.

I brought him home on July 9, 2007. He was a little over a year old. From the instant he arrived in my home, I just knew there was something very special about him. I knew that Sully was destined for great things.

For starters, we were already facing prejudice about his breed from my brother-in-law. He had never met a pit bull/pit bull mix and stated that he wanted my new dog to stay away from his dog and his family.

All it took to change his mind was to meet Sully. My awesome boy did all the rest.

He showed him that dogs should never be judged solely by their breed or by the way they look. His gentle nature, coupled with his love of people and other dogs quickly changed my brother-in-law's mind.

One done, many more to go.

With Sully being a pit bull mix, we had work to do to make sure he would always be an excellent breed ambassador. To do that, taking obedience classes together was first on our to-do list.

He was able to bypass the beginner class and jump right into the advanced class, which he passed with flying colors. The instructor took us aside after the final class and suggested that Sully would be an excellent therapy dog and we should look into doing that.

So it began. We started with getting his CGC (Canine Good Citizen) certificate, then on to the National Temperament Test, which he passed with highest honors.

Then we took the Therapy Dog Test, which we breezed through.

Sully is always happiest when he is making others happy!

Sully loves getting and giving kisses.

We have been a therapy team for over five years now and I am not sure who enjoys it more, me, Sully or the people he visits.

We not only visit hospitals and nursing homes, but occasionally we are asked to come to schools to teach appropriate behavior between little ones and dogs, as well as helping those that are scared of dogs find out just how calm and loving some dogs can be.

It only takes a minute for Sully's love to shine through and kids are soon opening up to him.

Why is Sully my hero?

Sully is my hero for many reasons. There are too many to list, but I will name a few.

His love for all humans, big or small, and the enthusiasm for which each and every person is greeted, makes me swell with pride and love for him.

Sully has been the best big foster brother to over twenty dogs and puppies. This is a task he does without any jealousy.

He gladly shares me, his toys, treats and even his best buddy, Ava, with nary a blink of his eye.

How did I get so lucky?

This boy is my love, my life and my best friend. He has proven to many pit bull naysayers that bully breeds are not what you hear or see on television.

We tell people we encounter that although we understand your fear, if you have never met a pit bull/bully breed to please just give them a chance. Meet just one and your mind may be changed.

Sully is my first pit bull, but by no means will he be my last.

He has changed my focus in life and I will always be grateful to him.

My motto is, the best defense against the anti-pit bull crowd is to have a well behaved pit bull in public.

Sully will always be a shining example of an awesome breed ambassador. He is truly my hero.

Update: In June, 2015, Sully welcomed a new pittie sister Keela. They are best friends.

CLANCY (LIZ, ADAM, REBOUND HOUNDS RESCUE)

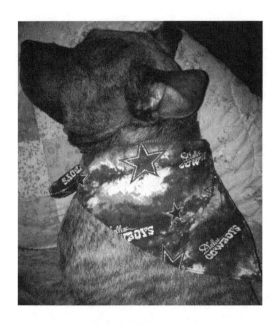

JAKE

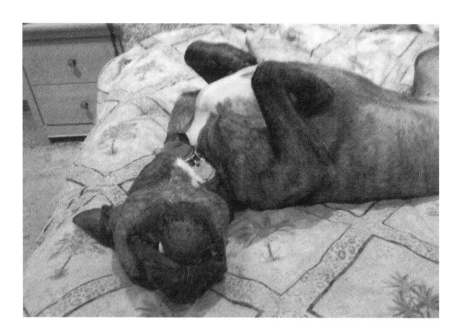

JAKE CONT'D (ALEX DASILVA)

CHANCE

CHANCE CONT'D (KATHY LEE RANDALL)

TYKA (UPDATE) – THANKS TO BETH CITURS

Tyka is doing well. She is now three years old.

She doesn't have any new siblings, just the two canine and four feline siblings she has always had, but we would like everyone to know about all of the foster siblings she has had - there are lots.

These are pictures of her with just a few of them. Best girl ever!

JOKER (AGATA COTA)

LEIA

LEIA CONT'D (ALLY D'ANDREA)

LUNA

LUNA CONT'D (KAITLYN COSTA)

MONTHLY HERO MISSY – THANKS TO CHANNIE KAHAN

One day my dad was driving home from Temple and saw a small black dog roaming the streets near our home. He stopped and got out of the car to try to catch her but there was no need. She jumped right into his car and, since there was nowhere else for her to go, he brought her home.

My mom said we could not keep her. At the time we had a full house with three dogs and five cats. I tried not to get too attached to her. That was very hard as she was adorable, sweet, funny and always happy.

We called her Missy. Our neighbors wanted her to be their guard dog. They would have kept her outside her whole life. We said no.

My mom finally decided that we could not give her away. She was certain that Missy would not be treated right by anyone else but us. She was so friendly and loving that my mom was a little insulted when we took her to the vet to get her spayed. Missy just walked off with the vet tech, never looking back at us and wagging her tail as she strolled away. My mom may have been insulted, but that is what I loved about her the most – her friendliness, her sweetness and her loving heart.

The first year we had Missy all we did was laugh constantly. She was the greatest joy in our lives. She had a funny way of walking with her cute little butt swishing left and right. She would sleep with me in my bed and would push me almost all the way off the bed so that she could have all the space to herself. When I would call for her she would come running as fast as she could, jump up wherever I was and knock me down with kisses and hugs.

Missy quickly became best friends with one of our older dogs named Ginger. Ginger was not impressed by Missy at first. Missy was a puppy and very playful. She nagged Ginger to play until finally Ginger relented. They became inseparable, playing and eating and sleeping together.

In 2006, my mom was diagnosed with cancer. She spent most of the year in the hospital. She had chemo and radiation, lost her hair, had no appetite and was very weak. It was a very sad year. I cried many times in Missy's fur and she was always there for me to give me big wet kisses and let me know she loved me.

Missy loved every single person she ever met. She loved all the cats in the house too. We also used to feed about twenty feral cats that lived in our backyard. Missy loved them all and they loved her. She was always happy to make new friends. Also, amazingly Missy never growled. I don't think she knew how. A cat could be swatting her and she just sat there. Missy did not have a mean bone in her body.

When my mom died, it was very hard for me. It was Missy who kept me alive. She was so pushy with her love, she would not take no for an answer. She stayed with me, loved me and kissed me every day when she saw me crying for my mom. She was always there for me.

After Ginger died, Missy was sad and lonely. We decided to adopt a dog from a rescue group, a little Jack Russell Terrier that had been abused and neglected. She was named Sierra and when we were first introduced to her, she would not make eye contact and had no interest in us. When she saw Missy though, her whole face lit up. They kissed each other and right away I knew Sierra belonged with us. Sierra made Missy young again. And Missy brought Sierra out of her shell. They played together, slept together and their favorite pastime was kissing each other.

Last August, Missy did not feel well. She wasn't eating and slept a lot. Then her belly got swollen. I took her to the vet and he gave me some medication. The day before my birthday, August 20th, Missy seemed to be in real pain and discomfort. I was getting ready to make dinner and the look on Missy's face froze my heart. She sat, then stood up, then she laid down. Then, after taking a few gasps of air, she passed away. I was sitting on the floor with her and she died right there and there was nothing I could do to help her. My girl was gone. We buried her in our back yard.

Missy's passing was very sudden. Nobody wants to see family members go, especially when one thinks that there is always more time to enjoy each other's company. At the very end she was with me, in her house surrounded by those who loved her. I believe she crossed over the "Rainbow Bridge" to be with other loved ones. Missy had the heart of a champion - a huge heart full of love and she gave that love to everyone she met.

I hope and pray that Missy is with my mother in heaven and that I will see them again one day. Not a day goes by that I don't think of that sweet girl and cry for her. She was always there for me, no matter what. She was my hero. My mom and Missy will always have my heart.

JEFFREY THE POSITIVELY PEACEFUL PIT BULL

Finally, I would like to share the story of a most extraordinary dog I had the honor of meeting in November, 2014. His name is Jeffrey and his accomplishments are nothing short of remarkable. Among his achievements, Jeffrey is an American Kennel Club Canine Good Citizen, a Registered Pet Partners Therapy Dog, a Reiki Attuned Canine, a Rally Obedience Competitor and an ambassador for shelter dogs everywhere.

Things began rather bleakly for Jeffrey. He was an eleventh hour rescue from death row at a high kill New York City shelter in August, 2010. "Ranger," as he was called at the shelter, had been abandoned in a park and brought to Manhattan Animal Care and Control by a park ranger. He quickly caught the dreaded shelter cough, was sent to the sick ward and was slated for euthanasia.

His now mom Michele had seen his photo on a Facebook page called Bruised Not Broken. She shared his post in hopes of helping him find a home. As she hit the "share" button, she received an intuitive jolt that directed her back to his photo. Something deep inside was telling her that she and this dog belonged together. She already had Sara Brown, a 10 year old Cattle Dog mix and had not been looking for another dog, but now Michele knew her little family would be expanding.

Brooke Slater of Bruised Not Broken put her in touch with two extraordinary shelter volunteers, Jeff Latzer and Carol Rothschild. Both played an integral role in saving Jeffrey, as well as Jeffrey's "Fairy Dog Mama," rescuer Samantha Bloom. If it were not for the love and commitment of these individuals, Jeffrey would not be here today.

If you haven't guessed, Jeffrey is named after Jeff. What most people do not know is that Jeffrey also has a middle name – Carol. Jeffrey and Michele continue to have a relationship with Jeff, Carol, and everyone else involved with saving his life. They are forever family.

Jeffrey and Michele quickly developed a deep, special bond. They enjoyed working together and Jeffrey possessed a strong desire to please. Training became part of their daily routine. Jeffrey was quickly ready to take his American Kennel Club Canine Good Citizen test, and he passed with flying colors. The examiner (Jeffrey Sochrin) told Michele, "This dog is so special. It would be crime if you did not pursue therapy work. This dog has what it takes." Mr. Sochrin has also become a beloved member of Jeffrey and Michele's extended family. He has even made Jeffrey an honorary member of Team Golden Dog, his rescue on St. Maarten.

Michele began to look into therapy work, researching different registries to find one that was well respected and stringent in its testing process. She decided to go with Pet Partners, formerly Delta Society. The training program was extensive. First Michele had to study and take a test. Next, Jeffrey was assessed. Finally, they were tested together. Jeffrey quickly passed the test and became a Registered Therapy Dog.

Jeffrey took to therapy work immediately. His sweet temperament, soft, soulful eyes and deep emotional intelligence made him a natural. Everyone he meets is a friend but he seems to have a special bond with children. His childlike nature and gentle demeanor draw children to him like moths to a flame.

Jeffrey has visited schools, college nursing programs, scout troops, nursing homes and Connecticut Hospice. He became a registered Reading Education Assistance Dog (R.E.A.D.) and has worked in an inner city library, providing a supportive listening ear to young readers. He visits a wonderful program called Integrated Refugee and Immigration Services (IRIS) teaching dog safety to children new to this country. Many of these children have never even seen a live dog before.

He and Michele have coordinated with a local veterinary hospital for humane education and dog safety programs. They teach responsible ownership as well as lessons on reading body language and proper ways to interact with dogs. Jeffrey's specialty though, is his work with grieving children. He is now in his fourth year with The COVE Center for Grieving Children and Families, and next year will be his fourth year at Camp Erin Connecticut. This program was brought to the State of Connecticut by the Moyer Foundation following the tragedy in Sandy Hook, where Jeffrey also served providing comfort and hope and building lasting relationships.

Witnessing Jeffrey interact with a grieving child is nothing short of magical. He intuitively knows exactly what each child needs. The child that needs a clown gets the wiggly, happy Jeffrey. Children needing a quiet shoulder get exactly that, a safe place to lay their heads and whisper their secrets.

Working with grief can weigh heavily on one's heart. To keep Jeffrey emotionally healthy, he and Michele enjoy Rally Obedience. Jeffrey always loves learning new things and what started out as a hobby has grown into a competitive endeavor. He also participates in behavioral studies at the Yale University Department of Canine Cognitive Behavior Studies.

Each December, Michele holds "Jeffrey's Joy of Giving," a donation drive that benefits the Norma Pfriem Urban Outreach Initiative, STARelief and Pet Assistance, A Hand for a Paw, and Beyond Breed Ruff Riders Program.

Giving back to the community is very important to Michele and Jeffrey. It is one more way to show gratitude for the many blessings that Jeffrey has received.

The bond that Jeffrey and Michele share is undeniable and profound. As a team, their mission is to gently spread peace and love, to teach by example that kindness is important. The human-animal bond is an extraordinary thing to witness and the love between the two of them is a joy to behold.

Jeffrey has appeared on television as a guest on Lauren Collier's Pet Talk Show and was a guest on the Channel 12

News. He was filmed for a documentary about Bruised Not Broken, the New York City advocacy group responsible for saving his life, as well as a piece filmed at the New York University School of Social Work about Animal Assisted Therapy. He was also the subject of a mini-documentary piece that appeared on MSNBC and the TODAY Show. He appeared on the cover of American Dog Magazine and was written about in The Huffington Post and in Dog Fancy Magazine.

CharlieDog and Friends LLC., a toy company in Rye, New York, has even made a stuffed version of Jeffrey. The company donates a portion of each purchase to local non-profit animal charities. The current beneficiary is Kim Wolf's Beyond Breed Ruff Riders Community Support Program, which helps people with basic necessities and veterinary care so that beloved pets can remain in their homes.

Not bad for an abandoned pit bull who was saved at the last minute from certain death! Jeffrey is living proof that shelter dogs are not damaged, just richer in life experience and deserving of a second chance.

Jeffrey has a special way of melting away barriers. Occasionally, Jeffrey and Michele meet someone who is fearful or has preconceived judgments about dogs that look like Jeffrey. Michele will always strike up a polite conversation with such individuals, acknowledging their fears and always treating them with respect. Trying to understand from the other person's point of view and meeting on common ground tends to be a great way to connect and these conversations almost always end in new friendships. To see a person let go of an overpowering fear and interact with Jeffrey is a beautiful thing. It is a precious moment in time where love shows its true power.

Jeffrey is a living lesson in grace and resilience. He is a beautiful example of how to live in the moment, love freely and embrace the interconnectedness of us all.
In the end, the simple truth is we are all just walking each other home.

https://www.facebook.com/Jeffrey-The-Positively-Peaceful-Pit-Bull-577254038955255/timeline/

Media links;
http://www.today.com/video/rescued-pit-bull-offers-comfort-as-therapy-dog-44411459813
http://www.huffingtonpost.com/2013/08/26/emma-wishneski-_n_3817953.html
http://www.examiner.com/article/death-row-pit-bull-shatters-stereotypes-and-befriends-sandy-hook-student
http://www.huffingtonpost.com/arianna-huffington/on-the-importance-of-appr_b_4592546.html

MICKEY

"I am so glad that you are here... It helps me realize how beautiful my world is." ~ Goethe

Mickey has had quite the year.

He has been a foster brother on four different occasions.

He has made some new friends and spent time with old ones.

He has visited many places –

Stores (where there are always treats waiting for him):

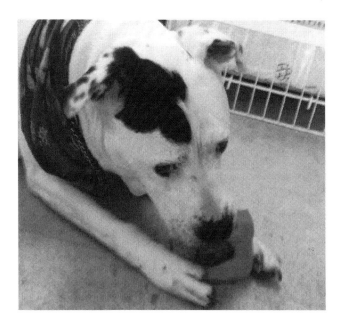

State and local parks:

Hiking trails:

Outdoor restaurants:

Beaches:

Universities:

Unusual places that many do not know exist:

He has met lots of new people and changed a few minds:

He is more confident and trusting every day and makes new friends wherever he goes. He is still a bit fearful, but he welcomes any new human and canine guests into our home with open paws.

Although he has his breed working against him and some people who don't know him are afraid of him, he is universally loved by all who take the time to know him.

I have no reservations about bringing him to visit elderly relatives, he is wonderful with children and he is hands down the sweetest dog I have ever had.

We still have some work to do but he has come such a long way. I could not be prouder of my boy!

Mickey continues to amaze me every day and I look forward to more fun times with him in the years ahead. I could never have predicted how much this boy would change my life for the better.

As always, my advice to anyone wanting to add a dog to the family is: Adopt a shelter dog – the life you change the most may just be yours.

ACKNOWLEDGEMENTS

To all who contributed, purchased or otherwise supported "Loyalty Unleashed: Pit Bulls and the People Who Love Them."

To all of my family and friends who have supported me and continue to support me in my writing, advocacy and rescue work.

To Dawn Harden of Floral Greens Publishing. "Loyalty Unleashed" would not have been possible without your help and support.

To Theodora DeBarbieri for all of your support, both personally and through print and television media.

To all who contributed to this book. Every dog has a story to tell. It is an honor to tell yours.

To those who have opened their minds and hearts to shelter pets of all breeds and species.

To those involved in rescue and those who volunteer their time to help homeless animals.

To pit bull lovers and dog lovers everywhere.
Thank you!

And a very special thank you to Jackie Seal and Phyllis Pasternak for their expertise in editing and proofreading.

"Last, I would like to thank the dogs…simply for being dogs, which is to say, tolerant and perseverant; willing to connect with a world that does not always return their affection; and for proving, time and again, that life, while messy, difficult, and imperfect, has the capacity to exceed our expectations and feed our undying hope." ~ Jim Gorant

Made in the USA
Middletown, DE
25 October 2016